Rivers Of Gold

Andrew Goldan Hawkes

Rivers of Gold; How to Create Multiple Income Streams
Copyright © Andrew Hawkes 2011
www.RiversOfGold.com.au

First Published in Australia 2015 by Goldan Group pty ltd
Copyright © 2011

® All rights reserved. No part of this publication may be reproduced or transmitted by any means, electronic, photocopying or otherwise without prior written permission of the author.
www.AndrewHawkes.com

ISBN-10: 0-9942799-0-6

ISBN-13: 978-0-9942799-0-3

All the information, ideas, techniques, skills and concepts contained in this publication are of a nature of general comment only and are not in any way recommended as individual advice. The intent is to offer a variety of information to provide a wider range of choice now and in the future, recognizing that we all have widely diverse circumstances and view points. Should any reader choose to make use of the information contained herein, that is their decision, and the author (and his companies) and publishers do not assume any responsibility whatsoever under any circumstances. It is recommended that the reader obtain their own professional advice.

"I am a person who likes a great quote – one that is thought provoking. Here is how Andrew starts the book: "The World will recognize You when You recognize Yourself." And with each chapter that follows we are presented with a quote to "hear" - that will ask us to listen to thoughts that may seem familiar and yet not implemented or discovered. This book is a must read for anyone that is ready to try a new approach and create a better version of yourself".

Ty Bennet
Speaker & Best Selling Author
www.TyBennet.com

"Simple, clear & imperative reading for anyone looking to diversify their income."

Rossco Paddison
Heart Centered Money Maker
www.hcmm.today

Acknowledgements

This Book is Dedicated to all the people who believed in me, the people who backed me in the writing phases and the 'will I, won't I publish it' phases.

To my children, Victoria, Harlyn and Emerson who inspire me to be a better person each day and continually teach me new ways to love and have fun. To my parents who gave me all that I needed in life to contribute to society in a useful way, to my siblings who have always given me reason to push further, harder, longer. To the Universe for providing me the platform and knowledge that enabled the writing of such a piece.

To my beautiful loving wife, Sarah, who always encourages me to look at things in another light. Thank you.

And to you, you who is reading this book. Thank you for trusting in me enough to get your own copy.

Use the information you find useful, and forget what you don't. I know the power of what is written in these pages, and it is because of you that it is written. Enjoy.

v

Rivers of Gold;
How to Create Multiple Income Streams

Andrew Goldan Hawkes

Table of Contents

FOREWORD 1

YOU SAID WHAT? 7

CONTROL YOUR MIND, CONTROL YOUR DESTINY 19

GETTING CLEAR 35

    S.I.M.P.L.E. Goals™   44

THE UGLY TRUTH 51

TYPES OF INCOME 67

MULTIPLE INCOME STREAMS 81

RIVERS OF GOLD 99

PACKAGING YOUR KNOWLEDGE 113

    Option One   116

Option Two	123
Option Three	125
Getting Your Product	130

GETTING ONLINE 131

Your Own Website	138
Your Landing Page, the Squeeze.	139
The Offer (Sales Page)	141
Thank You Page	143
Web Property	144

GET READY? BE READY! 147

4.5 TRILLION REASONS WHY 157

HOUSE KEEPING 169

Common Misunderstandings	170
The Wealth Paradox	173
You Are On Your Own	175

FINAL THOUGHTS 177

PRAISE FOR RIVERS OF GOLD 181

ABOUT THE AUTHOR 185

RESOURCES	187
The 10 Step Money System	187
Your Powerful Intention Audio	188

x

FOREWORD

"The World will recognise You when You recognise Yourself".
~Andrew Goldan Hawkes

Rivers of Gold is born from an innate desire to help as many people as possible who are willing to break the cycle of a poverty mindset, by teaching and educating participants about, not only making money by multiple income strategies, but also by showing them ways to protect themselves from the traps and to protect and grow their money through diversification and protection strategies.

From experience I know that making money can be, and indeed is, simple. However unless you have a method, or more importantly, a knowledge on how to maintain and look after that money, it will fall through your fingers like the desert sands.

I have also found that when one basic need is met and taken care of, a whole new world of creativity and freedom opens up that was not possible previously. A lot of this can come down to mindset.

For many years I have asked of myself the same questions over and over again, the ONE thing that kept coming up again and again was the fact that I myself had an inherent depth of knowledge that I was unaware of. This is a knowledge that I believe EVERYONE has an access to once they understand their true power. How then to tap into that power?

It is something that does take practice; to some it will come very easily and to others a little harder. It really comes down to how much exposure the individual has had to a particular way of thinking.

Again this all means nothing, this way of thinking, until that *one basic need* is met. Until this need is met an individual may experience moments of brilliance, and they may seem to last longer and longer each time and to be fair they probably are, as that 'muscle' is being strengthened. Then something will come up that automatically snaps us back to our indoctrinated way of thinking and we wonder *what the hell, and why the hell*, we thought that we could shine our brilliance in the first place.

I know this, as it was a cycle I lived for many years.

We are, and always will be our own worst critic. We all too often overlook our greatest achievements, mostly because we have been taught to listen to people who hold some mythical power e.g. teachers, parents, people of status and yes that includes the (seemingly) popular students at school.

I was recently back home at my parents and had a chance to reflect on my teenage years, that awkward time when we are finding out who we are, or more accurately, what society expects us to become, which of course can be anything from a homeless person on the street to a politician. My 6th form Dean told me that I was not *academically qualified* enough to join the Royal New Zealand Air Force, that I was wasting my time applying. I proudly served almost 11 years for my country and completed 5 tours of duty peacekeeping; imagine if I had listened to her.

While I was home I found some Surf Lifesaving competition medals, there were all three varieties, Gold, Silver and Bronze. I was an extremely capable athlete, yet ALL of my peers would have me believe that I was fat and good at NONE of those things.

Imagine if just ONE person had believed in me and *held me to a higher standard*, what could have been possible?

The important thing to get from all of this is that I could sit around and say 'what if?', or I could recognise that I still have that same potential, however, now it can be used in different ways to improve my life, my family's life and the lives of the people I have the pleasure of interacting with.

As I sat there with my competition medals I understood how hard I, and indeed how hard, ALL people are on themselves. It was in that moment that I began to realise my own TRUE worth and I began to cry, my wife knew why but my mother thought it was due to a lack of support from them over the years, but nothing could be further from the truth.

I unconsciously made a decision that day that I was worthy and capable of everything that I was dreaming and planning and I unconsciously gave myself permission to BE me, to BE myself and insist that all the people I associate with do the same.

So the one thing, *that one basic need* that when met makes all the difference is the KNOWING that all your weekly, monthly and yearly expenses are met. When this is accomplished magic happens. Simply by recognizing that I gave myself permission to simply BE me, I unconsciously began to attract all the resources that were needed in order for me to meet that *one basic need*.

It frees us to make clearer decisions, it allows us to be totally free to create. Totally free to BE authentically us – who the universe, the divine or whatever label you want to give it – meant for us to be.

I have met some amazing people on my journey, I have also met some complete assholes – although that could come down to the headspace I was in at that time. I look forward to the people that I am yet to meet who will impact my life – in any form that comes.

All you need to remember are three things… ***Learn, Act, Empower***

NAMASTE

YOU SAID WHAT?

"A person hears only what they understand".
~Johann Wolfgang Von Goethe

So I was lying in bed and it came to me, isn't that when most of your good ideas come? Like you are just drifting off into *'lala land'* a boom! IDEA! No way you can sleep now right? I could have gone back to sleep and hope that I'd remember the single most brilliant idea that I have ever had… ok maybe not the single most brilliant idea, however it rates right up there!

I have to say, ideas have always come pretty easy to me, I am sure you can relate to that. The human mind is a very precise and sophisticated machine that is far more advanced than most people tend to want to believe. I say *'want to believe'* as it is so much easier for people to plead ignorance and say that something is outside of their possibility. However that is all covered when we talk about mindset.

Seriously though, ideas come easy to you right? Well they should. Remember as a kid you were always up to something, there was always some big adventure. Unfortunately as adults we are indoctrinated by society and a high majority of us eventually conform to what is 'expected' of us. And for 90% of the earth's population this is unfortunately the way they live out the balance of their existence.

They lose, or rather, *restrain* that creativity and that becomes the basis for their ultimate failure. I am not saying that people *set out* to become failures, or even wind up with nothing as a career choice. I am simply pointing out that conforming to what others think and letting go of the child at heart is where it all begins.

It seems to me that there is some sort of disparity between the people that 'have shit' (stuff) in this world and the people that don't.

Society, you know media, friends, family, government, they would all have you believe that it is due to the fact that there is really not *enough* money.

Heck you could certainly be forgiven for thinking that in the US's case as they simply keep printing it, devaluing it by the day, and it has been going that way for quite some time, it is only now that we are about to witness the greatest wealth shift ever in the history of mankind and all of this means absolutely NOTHING to the uniformed, to the uneducated, to the main stayers of society.

When I am talking about the uneducated, keep in mind that I am not talking about the people who don't necessarily have a college or university education, and I am most certainly not talking about you, after all you have taken the time to purchase and read this book.

Well at least are you reading it… it may be a little presumptuous to think that there are not pirate copies of this out there, as this is the age we live in, you know what, if it is a pirated copy and you learn something from it that you can profit from then great, hit me up on my blog at www.AndrewHawkes.com and let me know about your success, I would love to hear about it!

I said we are about to witness the greatest wealth transfer in the history of mankind. I would love to say that I came up with that little gem all on my own, however my parents taught me to always speak the truth… so alas I did not .

I do think that it is very real, and to a bigger extent, friggin terrifying. Not for the reason you might think however.

Just in case you missed history class let me lay it down for you like this, remember the 1930's? There was this little thing that happened then where people were jumping off 40 story buildings due to the debt they owed (I know that feeling right?), of course history remembers it as *The Great Depression*. Up until this point in time, it has been known as the *greatest wealth transfer in history*.

You may have heard the little cliché that says *"History never repeats"*.

Well I am here to say, what a load of bullocks!

History repeats all the time - there are no *original* mistakes, they have all been made before.

Sure they may have a slightly different punch line, however, if you look closely you can see the same plot playing out time after time.

Rest assured, history repeats all right, we just tend to put a different spin on it. Even the great NOSTRADAMUS knew that history repeated itself, how else do you think so many of his quatrains were considered to be accurate? He was an avid study of the past. It has been said that all you need do to predict the future is to look to the past.

You wouldn't hear this on, or through the media, or from the government, to be honest they haven't the slightest clue (at least that is how they act..). Seriously, if the government had any clue at all they would be running the country like a business. They would have assets that are creating income from other countries, and this would eliminate the need to tax the people. How popular would they be then?

The truth is there are not a whole lot of competent people looking after your country, and this is accurate for most countries around the world.

Is there a solution? Of course there is... is it simple? Of course it is... could it be implemented? Most certainly it could... will it be? Not a chance!

So if there is a solution and it is simple, and it could be implemented, why then is it not being done? There are four main reasons that I can see for this;

1. It would take more than one term in power to accomplish, and even though it would be the right thing, and progress would be being made, people are so fickle and short sighted that they would overthrow the government before it had a chance to truly work and the opposition would sell off the assets to try to appease society.

2. It would highlight immediately any incompetence there might be at ministerial level, and it would force them to take responsibility (and no one wants to take responsibility)

3. It would prove (initially) to unpopular among the voters.

4. The Power brokers who truly run the world would lose to much control over the populous.

But wait; didn't I say that this would mean that the government could possibly cut taxes totally? Yes I did. However initially there would be things that the people might have to cut back on, and like anything, we as humans don't like to wait.

I have seen an example of this in the past. The country I will always call home, New Zealand, started doing exactly this in the early 1980's I was but a boy, and I most certainly did not understand it at the time, in fact I didn't truly understand it until recently.

While reading a Kiyosaki and Trump book *'Why We Want You to Be Rich'*, it all fell into place and made perfect sense. I truly believe that New Zealand would be an independently wealthy country had all the *'think big'* plans been left in place to grow to fruition. The only thing we can wonder now is 'What if?'

The reason I make such bold statements about cutting taxes totally, is that tax is a *relatively* new phenomenon and only actually became a regular thing in the mid 1800's.

I know, but what about the greedy Kings of old, you always see that they were over taxing their people and blah, blah... This is another one of society's tricks. Of course it is in their favour for you to think that wealthy people are tyrants, that way *psychologically* (and unconsciously) you won't really want to become one.

The truth is something totally different of course. In the past when people were paying their taxes to the king, they were in fact paying a lease of sorts so that they could work the land that the aristocracy owned so as to make a living for themselves and their families.

Initially when the government taxed its people it was to fund wars. So I guess you could say if you stopped the war then you would stop the tax... of course this then leads into wars stimulate the economy, and that is a book in and of it self.

With that in mind let me say that anyone can, and really should create multiple income streams. First however you must know where your money is going and how to grow it. The immediate issue with that is that most people don't know where to begin, so this is, in part where this book comes in.

Throughout this book I intend to show you where and how that you too can tap into some of the hundreds of income streams that are out there just waiting to be tapped. As Christopher Howard says 'It is never a matter of resources, it is a matter of resourcefulness.

So what can you expect from me? From this book? Well I am going to be totally honest with you… I have not always got it right. In fact I have had, what most people would call (as that is what society has trained them to do) a fatal failure, I went bankrupt… OMG there I said it!

Now it is not something I shout from the rooftops (I just publish it in books), however it has been a part of my journey and shaped who I have become in life and in business. The world didn't end.

All I can say is that I am glad I got it out of the way before the greatest wealth transfer in the history of mankind, (I can tell you I would rather say that than type it!) so I am able to position myself for my share, and believe me there is plenty to go around, you just have to position yourself.

The things that I am going to be talking about here will more than likely *challenge the way you think about money* and where it comes from, and that is a good thing!

If you get nothing else out of this book except a new way of thinking then it was a great investment on your part and the book has been a success.

There is plenty of evidence throughout history that showed me that incredibly wealthy people have lost everything in bankruptcy and have still made it all back and then some, they tend to make more as they now have a better understanding of what they can and cannot do.

So I look for the evidence of what works for me and I use that… isn't that what we all do? Sure it is, however most people use it in a negative way, and really you always get what you focus on.

Focus on the negative… get more of it.

Focus on the positive… and you will get more of that!

So I haven't always got it right, yet there is always an element in everything I do that I get *mostly right*. And regardless of getting it right or wrong, if you always get up one more time than you have been knocked down then you are always going to be ahead of the game and in the best position.

So I was saying… you can expect honesty, you can bet your bottom dollar that I will tell you what I have tried, what has worked, what hasn't and why…

To be honest there is only a couple of reasons as to why a lot of what I have tried has not worked in the way I would have liked.

You see I *learned* from that, which now it puts me in this incredible position to be able to share what hasn't worked and why. To show you what to do to change the outcome that I originally had. It only comes down to a few things that we are going to cover.

Let me add a caveat here, there are things that you will read about, and learn here, where you will go out and make the exact same mistakes as I have. That is OK.

Society might tell you that you are stupid, or that by learning from others mistakes that you are destined *not* to make the same ones. This is a fallacy as we can never *truly* get someone else's lesson without experiencing it.

It kind of gives us a sense of *'oh this is what Andrew was talking about in his book'*. It gives a map, of sorts, navigate where we are at any given time in our journey.

What can you expect from the book, well it is not a magic bullet... that is a blender... (bad joke, sorry). What I mean is that *just reading* this book is not going to magically make you a master of your own world.

And therein lies your first lesson. Think of it this way, going to church on a Sunday doesn't make you any more a Christian, than standing in a garage makes you a car. Get it? You actually have to do something, now there is a novel thought.

You should expect to come away from this book with;

- Efficiently track and measure your money movements.
- Begin to manage your money in a smart way that creates leverage.
- An understanding of why most other people fail
- How to avoid doing just that
- How to attract just the right circumstances into your life
- How to master your destiny once and for all
- An Understanding of the different types of money
- The belief that you too can have multiple streams of income

It is important to me that you get something of value from this book, sure there are other books out there that can show you this stuff.

There are websites all over the show that will tell you they can show you how, and they probably can... in my experience all of the websites that claim to teach you what you are about to learn in here are looking to sell you their products that does it all for you.

That is not saying that there is nothing else for sale here as there no doubt will be. However the information that you are going to get here you will definitely be able to go out and uncover your hidden rivers of gold by yourself, you will have the skills and confidence that you need in order to succeed.

No need to invest in anything else, all I am saying is there may well be options to.

With that, I think it is about time that we dive into the next chapter, and by the time you are done with that you will have the power to read minds and use the Jedi mind trick... ok probably not... we can have some fun with it though.

See you on the next page

CONTROL YOUR MIND, CONTROL YOUR DESTINY

"All that we are is a result of what we have thought, the mind is everything. What we think, we become"
~Buddha

Everywhere you look these days you can see it. Hold on, maybe *you don't*. Do you see what I see?

Let me rephrase what I said; everywhere *I* look these days I see it, perhaps that is because I am open and aware to it.

Just for your information the body is bombarded by about two million bits of information per second, and through the internal filters and our mind *deletes, distorts, and generalises* the information. Then allows what we think is important (due to the sub conscious rules we create) through to our conscious thought, or conscious mind if you like. It breaks it down from two million plus pieces to just seven plus or minus two chunks.

So the reason I rephrased my statement into a question to you was for this reason;

Personally I am open to the information I am referring too, and as a result it shows up on my radar without me having to think about it consciously, conversely if you are not necessarily *'open'* to the information I am referring to, or your sub conscious mind does not believe it to be important then you may well not see it.

It has a name and it is called *'Perceptual Blindness'*, and to recap, it filters out information that does not fit with our model of the world.

Far out, what a heavy way to start the chapter. No one said it would be easy right? So bear with me, I promise you it will be worth your while.

What I was actually referring to when I made the original statement was this, there seem to be more and more self-help professionals popping up every day. More retreats, more gurus, more experts. And with good reason more and *more* people are beginning to realise that they need help and assistance, they need a little guidance.

The same as people who have been down the hard road have something to share; they are gaining new insights into ways in which they can give back, in ways that they can fill those basic human needs of connection and significance.

Why do you think this book is written?

Yes I have something to share, yes I think it has the power to make a difference in your life, be it through monetary gain, higher self-confidence, self-worth and a stronger mind.

I truly believe that what I am sharing with you here has that power, and if I did not believe it I would not be sharing.

You see I am the sort of person that really does try and do things the easy way… so writing a book, spending hours and hours proof reading it does not turn my wheels so to speak. Helping out and changing people's lives for the better does. So here we are.

The title of this chapter says it all really, and to be honest, it doesn't get any less complicated. We as humans are the ones who tend to complicate things… in fact we complicate everything. We are meaning creating machines, if something happens… well it must *mean* something.

With that basic understanding in mind we can consider that something only has the meaning that *we choose* to give to it. For instance;

You get a phone call from your best friend, and they sound a bit flat. Unbeknown to you, their grandmother has just passed away, your friend is stricken with grief (golly I used stricken in a sentence) and she is not dealing with it well.

She doesn't want to burden you with her issues. You end the phone call thinking, *'man that was weird; I wonder what I have done?'*

You see in that small example you automatically attached a meaning to what just happened on the phone without even giving thought to the fact that there may be something going on that you don't know about in your friend's life.

And this is what we do on a daily basis, I guarantee that if you were to survey and analyze your daily existence and routine that you could find at least one example… unless of course you are a guru yourself and control 100% of your thoughts.

I have been involved with personal development for many years and I can tell you that it still happens to me from time to time, in fact more often than it should. The thing that I have noticed with that is this, I am more affected, or put another way, I tend to attach meaning to something when I am emotionally involved in what is going on, i.e. when it involves a loved one or family member. This is when we are more likely to attach, or create a meaning to what is going on.

The reason that this is important to know is that is has everything to do with our ultimate success.

This book is about establishing the foundation for Multiple Income Streams. The subject matter of this chapter could (and has been done countless times) be a book on its own, with its own merit.

Yet there are some important principles that I need to touch on here that will ultimately determine your success or failure with any given task, be it making money, creating loving relationships, becoming an addict or living on the street.

I am speaking from experience when I say this to you; it is very possible for you to hold two opposing thoughts at the same time. I know this goes against a lot of what other experts might tell you, so let me break it down for you.

When the experts say that you cannot hold two opposing thoughts at the same time, they are in fact referring to the conscious mind, and to that I must concede, as of yet I have been unable to hold two thoughts simultaneously (my Jedi powers are *not yet* strong enough), let alone two opposing ones. With that in mind then, you must recognise that I am referring to the unconscious mind.

This is where it starts to become a little murky. There is a lot of literature out there that will tell you if you have mantras and positive affirmations that you can accomplish anything, and you can… however there is a *key* ingredient missing with that equation that will render it useless if left out, and we'll get to that in a moment.

Why when you see these people via testimonials and endorsements of a certain product or service touting of their unbelievable transformation, or amazing results offer the fact they used affirmations as the reason for their success?

Listen up, as this is something that plagued me for a very long time... for as long as I remember I have thought about success, I had dreamed about it, I had sensed it close, yet so far way. And it wasn't until I got this ONE thing that it all fell into place.

I studied under some of the most successful people in an extremely lucrative home based business, I did what they said, right down to the letter it seemed, yet I was not having the results that others were having. I was not having the results I *thought* I deserved.

I honestly thought that there was something wrong with me.

There are literally hundreds of blogs and websites online where you can read about the [1]BE DO HAVE so I am going against convention here and not including it, if you want to know more simply Google 'BE DO HAVE' *(if you enter the search term "be do have Andrew Hawkes", as I wrote it there, you will see my article on it)* and see what you come back with, everyone has their interpretation of it, and you know once you understand it, you too will have your own interpretation of it, and that is very cool.

---

[1] Be Do Have Included on Page 160

So there is this ONE thing. This ONE key that is missing from most everything that is taught. I say *most* everything... I mean I had to learn it somewhere right?

I didn't come up with this on my own, in fact I heard about it through 'The National College of Business' here in Australia, they pointed me in the right direction.

They introduced (metaphorically) me to a guy by the name of Simon Sinek, and if you are familiar with him, then you will know what I am about to say... if you are not, Google him too and you can read more in depth (or watch a video) about the ONE thing.

The key that has made ALL the difference to my success and massive turn around from being broke with no money, no things, no life, to being vibrant and youthful again, to having a MASSIVE reason for getting out of bed in the morning, to being able to provide my family with the sort of life I have promised them for years. And that ONE thing, that ONE key, is simply this... WHY?

Yes WHY?

So what has WHY got to do with controlling your mind, and to a greater extent controlling your destiny?

This is the missing ingredient, if you like, for most people wanting success yet not achieving it. Go ahead, go and read some biographies and check it out for yourself.

Almost all of the successful people throughout history were successful because they knew *why* they were doing what they were doing.

Right now you are quite possibly thinking… well duh…. I know I did. For years I was, yeah I know why I am in business; I know why I am doing this or that.

And what I found was that I really had no clue. I had inadvertently closed off my mind to the *new* understanding of why, I was going through the motions, and I was doing all the right things only I had no real understanding of why I was doing all of that, and for as much as its worth. Without the true essence of why you are doing something you might as well go and get a job.

Get that.

It is seriously that important, this book is about creating and uncovering hidden multiple income streams, and yet in the last sentence I told you if you don't truly get the essence of why, you might as well go and get a job.

Understand that, control THAT and you will control your destiny.

So how come it all changed for me? Well I made a choice, and I know that sounds so cliché, however it is the truth. One day I got sick and tired of living in the lie that I was telling myself daily, that I was touting on the social networks.

Externally I was portraying this confident charismatic individual with the world at my feet (and consciously I truly believed that.) Yet internally and subconsciously I was sick with disgust in what I was saying to others.

I wasn't an example, I was, as I say, living a lie, day after day, after day. Sure I was charismatic but I was in no way the confident person that I portrayed.

Did I give sound advice... you bet I did... was I following it myself? Ah NO, epic fail!

I was out of integrity with myself. I wanted to help other people, I wanted to share with them that it was all about how you looked at things, and that you can have anything that you desired. And yet this was not true in my life.

Yes all of those things are true, and yes I still want to share all of those things with people, however there was no credibility in what I was saying. I was incongruent.

Despite what you may think, it was not due to a lack of results, I mean I have had amazing results in the past, I was selected for a development squad to represent New Zealand at the age of 18 and I was not what you would call a prolific athlete.

In fact what I have just told you will more than likely come as a huge surprise to most of the people that I went to school with, I pretty much flew under the radar at school as I was not in any 'clique' I was not one of the cool kids. The funny thing about that is that all of that crap means nothing in the real world anyway!

I had also made plenty of money in the past, so no it was not due to a lack of results.

It was due to a lack of self-belief and a massive helping of 'beat yourself senseless' every time you do something partially wrong. Tell yourself that you are worthless and that it is no wonder you lost all your money.

Why would your family want you there? You know all of the really healthy stuff that makes you feel like you would be better off dead than fulfilling your true potential.

How sad that is, to know that people do this out of perpetual habit. I am sure you can relate though right?

Have we not all been down tough roads like this before? Yeah sure, and it is how we come back from this that determines our future, and that is a wonderful thing, and here is why… no one can control that except you.

OK so results weren't the reason there was no credibility… self-doubt was. I personally believe that this is the biggest reason why more people don't take more of a chance, or take their dreams and potential more seriously.

Yes fear does absolutely play a part in that, and yes I would even say that it is fear of success rather than failure. If they were successful in what they were about to do, then there would be nowhere to hide, they would be in total exposure to the world.

Now that the rest of the world knows them as this capable self-confident person, there is nowhere to shy away from the light. Perhaps this is why so many people who are "successful" fade away into obscurity… or maybe it is merely the fact they didn't fully understand *why* they were doing what they were doing.

If you have ever heard Tony Robbins speak, either in person or on his audios you will know that change happens in an instant, and that instant is when you decide.

Well for me it was more like a fluorescent light, you know the kind with a starter, and when you flick the switch it doesn't turn on right away? I could sense that something was changing, and this was due to the fact that I consciously knew that something needed to.

I wasn't getting the results I truly wanted and that meant that I had to get pretty honest with myself and make some tough judgment calls, my ego was finally abiding in me and allowing me to grow, I knew that I knew something however I didn't know what.

I had invested a lot of time learning and developing new strategies and techniques, not only for marketing and developing businesses and business ideas, but time developing me.

There is an old saying, that if you hang around a barber shop long enough you are going to get a haircut… well I guess metaphorically I had been in the barber shop for a little too long.

Let me see if I can give you an example of what I mean, if you have ever seen the movie 'the 13th warrior' with

Antonio Banderas in it then this will make sense to you, if not it is like being in a total immersion class when learning a language.

Basically in the film Antonio's character is seconded to an army. This army do not speak his language, they are at sea to make it to wherever the battle is.

During this journey the foreign language starts to become broken English, as he is learning more and more. Eventually the whole movie is once again in English, representing that he has learned the language of the army he was sent to fight with.

What I am saying here is that a lot of the things I knew I knew, I now know why. The more I was in the environment the clearer things became for me right up to the point where I was approached to partake in a business course provided by 'The National College of Business'.

You know when something just seems to happen at the exact right time? This was one of those times, and I have to tell you I am so grateful about the fact that it came when it did, though again, not for the reasons you might think.

So here I was with this entirely new skill set, and all of a sudden things started dropping into my lap, all of a sudden I was Johnny on the spot for all the right opportunities, things were turning up left and right, and they were in perfect synchronicity with the new direction I was heading.

So I start at this course with 'The National College of Business' and the first day turns out to be a duesy, to be fair at this stage I was still not sure of my why… I just knew something was changing and that things were aligning for my ultimate success.

It was on this day, that I really started to understand my why, and the totally stupid thing was it was not that far from what I thought it was, it was close, but not quite. That is why this exercise is SO important.

There was the usual anticipation of a new group of people that would ultimately have to introduce themselves to the rest of the group, let them know what it is you did in business and why, the usual stuff.

Throughout the day there were plenty of questions being raised, the lead coach for the business group was in fact getting an understanding of what people knew and at what level they were playing at.

This was the moment that I personally needed, and as moments go, it was a long one.

By the end of the first session I was totally on fire… I had finally got it; I finally understood what so many people had tried to tell me in the past.

I finally understood my true worth, and let me tell you it is an absolutely amazing feeling.

If you haven't yet experienced that for yourself, I am excited for you, you have much to look forward to, and if you have experienced it, wasn't it one of the most amazing things you have ever felt?

I am still excited for you too, as now you understand your value, and believe it or not, you can't put a price on that no one could ever pay you enough money for you to say 'You know what, I forget my self-worth, my value'.

The thought of it is absurd, how could you forget any way right? There is a way, but let's not dwell on that, focus only on what you do want, as opposed to what you don't want.

All right then, what is it that you must control to control your destiny, yes your mind. And how do we control that? We start with why.

Grab yourself a pen and paper and start right now. Ask yourself this question, and make sure that you actually write it down, there is an emotional connection that is almost inexplicable when it comes to writing things down on paper, it tends to drag out even more information once you tap into your subconscious part of your brain, and it is an inspiring thing. The question is this;

'Why do I get out of bed in the morning?'

Or, if you are in business,

'Why am I in business?'

Or, if you are looking to create extra income streams,

'Why do I want extra income streams?'

The first answer you get is more than likely going to be a bullshit answer, it is something your lazy ass conscious mind spits out to try and appease you and give you a false sense of accomplishment.

So when you get that BS answer then you can go right ahead and simply ask *'why is that important?'*

Eventually you are going to get to the real answer, and you will know... if you are doing this exercise with anyone else (by that I mean verbally asking and answering) you will start to choke up, if you are doing it by yourself you will start to get goose bumps as you start to get truly excited about the possibilities that you now understand are only a start date away.

And THAT is a beautiful thing.

So obviously mindset plays a hugely important role here... (Well duh) however it is more than affirmations and mantras, it is about truly getting to the core of who it is that you are, and WHY you do what you do.

Once you master this, then you really do master your destiny. Is it fool proof?

You can bet the farm on it.

Can you fall off the wagon?

Absolutely, and many people do, so mastering your mind set is not a one and done deal, it is something that you continually have to work at, it is something that you should give yourself permission to schedule in each and every week, and this is something we will talk about a little later on, I am going to share with you the exact same techniques and strategies (heck I am even going to share the tools themselves) that I use to keep myself, my relationships and my business running smoothly and sustaining rapid growth.

And of course you can use them too when you are developing your very own *'rivers of gold'*.

Now, I think that it pertinent here to slip in my caveat, all of this mindset stuff is good, and there really is only one key theme in this particular chapter, however, in all of my experience (which includes losing a million dollars' worth of cash and assets) and with all of the truly successful people that I have ever spoken to, it was never, never, NEVER about the money.

So if your why is so you can HAVE more money, then you have missed the point, and yes you may get that money, I assure you it will only be a very brief encounter. Any truly successful person that I know of, the money was for a 'bigger than me picture', that's not to say you shouldn't enjoy the spoils of it, merely that it shouldn't be your sole intention, and again I reiterate, if it is… you have TRULY missed the point.

So to cover off, there is something you need to do RIGHT now if you have not already done it, and that is to ask *why*?

GETTING CLEAR

"The more intensely we feel about a goal, the more assuredly the idea, buried deep in our subconscious, will direct us along the path to its fulfillment"
~Earl Nightingale

For years this is something that I struggled with, and to be fair most people that I know also have had their struggles with this.

In fact it could be argued that there are a lot of people in this world who still aren't really clear about what it is that they want to achieve in life. I say this simply as a reflection of the people that have unbridled success in this world, which would be roughly 3% of the world's total population.

Not a great deal of people, sure a reasonable number when you perhaps compare it to a country like New Zealand for example, yet when you break it down to the percentage then it really is not that flash now is it?

You are likely defending that in your head right now and you are saying to yourself that I don't know what I am talking about. So let me put this question to you... *are you exactly where you want to be in life?*

Is this what you saw for yourself as a child, I mean are you living the fairy tale that you thought out when you were younger? If the answer to this is no, then perhaps this is exactly what you need to hear. Or rather need to understand for you to be able to let go of some of the stuff you have been holding on to that has ultimately held you back.

Right now, there is also a little part of you that is saying that I am *naïve* to think that the fairy tales exists, or that it one might be foolish for thinking that they even could. So now to that I pose this question... *is this an attitude that you learned from society?*

Is it something your parents said? Or are you *cynical* due to the fact that you haven't made it yet?

What ever your reason or excuse, I would like to invite you to consider that this is perhaps why you have not yet achieved. In all my years of struggle, not once did I think that success would not happen for me or my family.

This chapter is really about getting clear, how can it be done. It is about providing you with solid tools and strategies for how to get totally clear on what it is that you want here in this time called life.

It has been said on many occasions and by many personal and professional development authorities that it doesn't particularly matter what the vehicle is that you use to achieve this outcome.

To an extent this is very true, I know of people that are extremely successful and fulfilled, that have done so through a particular vehicle that would not have been their first choice. However there is something very special about creating the success through a medium or vehicle that you are passionate about. And there are many ways in which you can achieve this.

Of course this all means nothing unless we are crystal clear about *why* it is that we are doing what we are doing. So the same as in the last chapter we really are talking about *why*, although now when we talk about our why are actually going to explore how the hell we can get clear about why.

The exciting part about this is that when we know the *"why"* the *"how"* shows up. Not only does it show up, it shows up in super fast fashion that you rarely have any control over.

Bear in mind that it might not show up in the form you expect, I mean you may have had an idea of what it was you were *meant* to be doing, and as we have discussed here, it may be *close* to what you think it is.

Yet I can almost guarantee that the how that shows up will surprise you like you wouldn't believe.

There are plenty of books out there that will teach you how to set goals. They will tell you the formulas that you can use, they put together clever little acronyms that all have great meaning and help you to focus on what you want to achieve. I have a slightly different train of thought, yes I still use goals, and I even have my own foowah (is that a word?) acronym for them. Yet before I get into that I think that it is important to understand why you would set one and the true anatomy of what a goal is really about (this is my take anyway).

To be able to set a truly accurate goal and have it come to fruition and bear the fruit that you desire you must first understand your end result. I am sure that I will not be telling you anything new when I say that you need to begin with the end in mind. This is again something that I struggled with, how can I start with the end in mind when everything in my conscious being was a stark reminder of poverty and lack thinking?

For your goal to become a reality (and reality is simply a construct in the mind) you must actually *believe* that you have *already attained* it on some level.

Simple right? Yet I am sure you would have set goals before (and if you haven't that is OK, it means you have no preconceived ideas), but have you always reached them?

There are two answers that could possibly come from this and both of them are lies.

What?

Yes, both of them are lies, you see there are things that we have achieved in life that we might not consider them as *goals*, yet somewhere in the timeline of your life you actually set out to achieve it. If you hadn't it would not have happened.

So then the flip side of that is the fact that some of the goals you say you have achieved, you are only telling half-truths about.

Don't get me wrong, this is not about making you right or wrong, it is merely highlighting the fact that the little voice inside our head sometimes tries to let us off the hook and allows us to deceive ourselves, *we* are the only one we deceive when we do this.

This is all good and well, however what does it have to do with getting clear about the outcome? To start with the end in mind, so therefore we are able to set goals to reach that end, we must be clear. So then let us now discover the tools to do exactly that.

There is a process that a company, or an individual, goes through in order to find their ideal target market when they are selling something. This exercise, or process, is one of writing an extremely detailed description of who they are selling too, what they wear, where they live, what sort of car they drive, are they male or female, do they have children, how old are they, and on and on.

This is an extremely powerful exercise for these companies and individuals alike, it enables them to build a pretty good idea of the person they want to talk to, it enables them to talk to a person's core.

So then what if we were to reverse that slightly and actually create a profile of ourselves, only ask the questions as to what would your ideal day look like? Where would you live, what would you be doing, would you use an alarm to wake up, are you into sport, would that be part of your day, are you of service to others, what would you be doing at any particular time of the day? There are plenty of questions like this that you can ask yourself to create what your perfect day would look like.

I guess it is important to mention here that for success to be lasting then it must be a bigger than you existence. I can certainly speak from my own experience, however I can also speak as an observer as well.

I know of a couple who were extremely successful, and while they were *of service* to others, and helped others succeed, the money flowed to them like water into the sea, this changed when they were no longer aligned with this and they began haemorrhaging money like an erupting volcano.

The level of your income or your lifestyle has a direct coloration with the level of service you provide the world. And the level of income and success you *believe* that you deserve.

That doesn't mean necessarily that you must go out and save the world, or be something that is a global phenomenon (although if your why is big enough that may end up happening).

One way in that you can start to get clear, what else can you do? Start to think about the things that you wanted to do when you were a child, was it that you wanted to sing or play music, perhaps you wanted to be a champion *grand prix* horse jumper.

Give yourself permission to be that child again, ask those questions that you always asked back then, there is so much power in that.

Here is something else you can do, grab a pen a paper (I'll wait). Now on the paper I want you to write these questions.

'What are the top five things that I am passionate about?'

'If I had the unlimited resources what would I do in those five areas?'

'What do I want people to say about me when I am done and dusted (dead)?'

Here is the trick with this, give yourself at least three A4 pages in which to answer **each** question.

You may be thinking, Andrew, three pages? There is no way I could fill that... I assure you that once you start writing and actually give yourself permission to just let it flow out that the three pages will more than likely not be enough.

Once you have finished reading this chapter start that, and keep writing until you think you are done.

Here is a tip;

if this is an exercise that you do not complete (as with the others throughout this book) then I would hazard a guess that this is why you are not yet achieving what it is you think you are supposed to be achieving.

By simply not following through with this simple activity you are demonstrating the fact that you are not willing to do what it takes to be successful beyond imagination (I know from experience that if you don't do it now... you NEVER will).

Once you have finished that exercise you will be starting to have an idea as to why you get up, as to what it is that perhaps you want to be doing that is a "bigger than you" idea.

For me writing this book is a "bigger than me" idea, and I am very clear as to why I am doing it.

By now you might be asking yourself, yeah, but Andrew, what does all of this have to do with Multiple Income Streams?

And to that I would answer in this way. The fact that you are willing to look at Multiple Income Streams as an option for yourself is due to the fact that you want something more out of life, with that in mind you owe it to yourself to be so crystal clear.

There are going to be days when you simply can't be arsed getting out of bed or even leaving the house, there are days when you are going to want to call in sick (you know you have done it before). It is during these times that when we are totally focused and crystal clear on what it is that we are doing and more importantly why we are doing it, that ultimately gives us the power to carry on, to get up at least one more time than we have been knocked down.

So in getting clear, we can take the insights that we have gained from the exercises that we did above. Then we can start to map out what that looks like and how long we think before we are getting close to where we think that should be.

I'll give you a tip here, we are always evolving (well at least we should be) and by the time you actually get to where it is that you *think* you should be, that will have changed.

I want you to know that is OK, ideas and concepts are allowed to evolve and grow with us, in fact, they *must* for them to have any chance of long term success and survival.

Let me share this, when I first got the idea for this book, it was just that, a book, and now already it has evolved into something even bigger, a series of books, each one exploring new ways in which to have your money work for you, as opposed to you working for your money.

So now, you've mapped out a time frame, great, you are clear as to why, now you can set your goals... you have a different feeling right? You actually feel empowered to get shit done; you actually have a *certainty* about why you are doing it. Great!

So my goals formula acronym goes like this; S.I.M.P.L.E. Goals™

Specific (Colour, type, size, year, refine your details - By when?)

Individual (As in YOURS, they must be YOUR goals)

Measurable (How will you know you are on track?)

Powerful (Do these goals provide you with a powerful desire to succeed?)

Likely (Is this a Goal that is likely to get you out of bed in the morning?)

Ecological/Enjoyable (Good for you, good for others, good for the environment, and you MUST enjoy it).

So let's delve a little deeper into these goals.

Specific:

In order for a goal to have its ultimate power and to be fully realised, not only does the 'big picture' have to be clear, the small steps in getting there, the goals, must be detailed and specific. Being vague about what you expect from your goal will get you a vague result. Let's walk through an example of what it is that I mean.

Say you are looking to make some extra money (fitting as this book is about the foundation of multiple income streams). You could say, (and believe me most of the masses do) *"I want more money"*.

Great, here is a dollar, now you have more money. Get that? (Not incredibly difficult right?).

That is precisely what nine out of ten people do. I guess to a greater extent that is why nine out of ten people are living in lack, or to put it a little more scientifically why 90% of all retirees are dependent on government handouts.

Let us look a little further into this example of money... how then would we make it more specific and meaningful? Good question right, and for you maybe this is something you already know, but then again it may not be.

You would word it in such a way that whoever picked up your goal and read it would know the exact amount of money you were looking to create or achieve, and more importantly why and by when.

I have a friend and author who had a goal to reach a specific goal of $20,000 a month. Now was he reasonable in obtaining that? Well by definition, no, he was not. In fact he effectively had to change his vocation in order for him to actually reach that goal, but reach it he did.

Now had he not been specifically clear about exactly how much he wanted to earn, he may have never taken the opportunity that lead him to not only making $20,000 a month, but it also took him on to being a self-made multi-millionaire and a top performer in his industry.

This of course is just one example of being specific, and it is most certainly something that you can play around with, the more *real and specific* you can make it, the more emotionally attached to it that you can become, the faster that it is going to actually show up in your life.

If I could offer an example of my own… to write a book has been a goal of mine for some time. The only issue was that I wasn't really sure what it would be about did I have something to offer people that would be of value? (And of course the answer is Yes!) So because of this lack of specificity then it took a little while for the wheels to get in motion, in fact the wheel had been turned a couple of times where other books were started.

 No it was not until I become crystal clear about when (and why) this book would be published, what it would include, that there would in fact be a follow up series with it that its really started to take on a life of its own. And to be honest, I really couldn't stop it now if I wanted to. That is the power about being specific in setting your goal.

Individual:

This is one that gets me, in fact you can see it in almost every Hollywood movie that hits the screens... well maybe not almost every, but certainly a high percentage. You know you have seen the ones I am talking about.

High school jock really wants to be a ballet dancer but his father wants him to be starting quarterback for the varsity side and then go on to play in the NFL, high school jock gives up his dream to please his father and then resents him for the rest of his life? (Damn, I should write Hollywood screen plays!)

It is kind of important to make sure that your goal is in fact your own, and it is not just because you will end up resenting the person whose dream it actually is... no it is WAY more important than that.

Think about this; how enthusiastic are you about doing something that is not your idea? I mean seriously, you might say *"oh yeah ok, let's go"* but you are not really interested, you sort of go along for the ride.

How different is the reaction when it is your idea, something of your creation? Don't you get a lot more excited? Sure you do (even if you won't admit it here, and you know what? It's just us, it is OK you can admit it).

The point here is this, if the goal is yours, if it is *individually* yours and no one else's you are 100 times more likely to follow through with it to the end, and as my friend Kurek Ashley says *"the fortune is ALWAYS in the follow through"*.

Measurable:

How will you know if you are getting close to, or even on track to reaching your goal? There must be milestones along the way that you can 'measure' it against.

When you measure and track how you are going you can make the necessary adjustments that need to happen in order for you to get to where it is you are going.

Don't make the mistake that many people make and use the measuring as a tool to beat yourself up when you are not on track… use it as it was meant, *to provide reference* for your ultimately achieving what it is that you have set out to achieve.

If you are not as close as you would like, be thankful that you are on your path at all. Always look for the things that are going right, this is how you will ultimately succeed.

Powerful:

This is where you can start to add the essence that will ensure your success in achieving your goal, no matter what.

Make the reference for your goal so immensely powerful that you can feel the feelings you will have as a result of you having gotten your goal.

It should be so powerfully written and described that the very mention of it gets you excited, this is what is needed to ensure that you carry on and push through any and all hardship that you may have on your road to achievement.

There will be times where the going gets hard. It is how you equip yourself to deal with that which will be the yardstick that you can measure against.

When you are *powerfully* connected with your outcome then you can push through and realise your goal and your own unique power to succeed.

Likely:

Now this one can cause confusion so make sure that you understand it. You must, and I mean *must*, stretch yourself if you are to grow and succeed. At the same time you must set a goal that has an achievable outcome.

What I mean by that, is you might be naive to think that you could set a goal to compete at the Olympics in the 100m sprint if you had trouble getting out of your house and walking to the letterbox.

That is not to say that you could not achieve the former, just that you would be wise to start with a goal closer to reality like walking, or even running a 100m first. Then work up to the Olympics, I mean who am I to say that you shouldn't set *that* goal… however I want you to achieve.

So the old adage goes, how do you eat an elephant? One bite at a time.

So there you go. Likely.

Ecological/Enjoyable:

Ok, so this one is a little of a double header. First up, your goal should excite you. It should be something that you are going to have fun with, something that is enjoyable to you, otherwise what is the point?

I mean really? Have fun! The other aspect to consider is ecology, which basically means that it should be good for the planet (not harm it), good for you, and good for your friends and family (again read not harm them).

That is *my* little acronym for Goals. I find it powerful and it has helped keep me on track, but look, use whichever one you are comfortable with.

I am not going to say I am right and the others are wrong, as that is far from the truth (and my ego is not that big). There will be people that this works for, and people that the others work for. Whatever one works for you, and you are comfortable with, is the *right* one.

THE UGLY TRUTH

"All truths are easy to understand once they are discovered; the point is to discover them".
~Galileo Galilei

Great chapter title right? It smacks of contempt and intrigue, and to be fair there may be a little contempt in there.

I have to warn you, this chapter is a little 'heavier' than I would have liked, I looked at ways in which it could be made a little lighter and a little less lecture like, unfortunately it is information that needs to be shared and there is no other way to put it. At least not from my stand point anyway. It is what it is, just realise that it is information that you need to know.

When I speak about the *ugly truth* I am referring to what the government in most countries don't really elude much to. They know that there is an issue, yet they seemingly do nothing about it.

I say this due to the fact that the statistics have not changed in over 60 years, in fact if you were to take a poll now I am sure you would find that the statistics are in fact being far *too kind* to the stark contrast in reality.

What are the statistics that I am referring to? Well Earl Nightingale spoke of these in his well-known and highly regarded *'The Strangest Secret'* audio that he created for his team members, he said;

'If you were to interview 100 people at the age of 25 and then again at the age of 65. 25 of them would be dead, 54 will be DEAD broke living off government family or friends, 16 will be living just above average, they will need to supplement their income (super, pension, benefit etc...) four will be financially independent and only ONE will be independently wealthy'.

If these statistics have been around for over 60 years, and have not really changed that much, we must ask the logical question as to why not, right?

It would be easy to sit around like an ostrich with our heads in the sand, and to be fair many of us have. Please don't

Age 25   Age 65

- **25 Are Dead**
- **54 Are Dead Broke, living of Family, friends or Government benefits**
- **16 Are Living Just above Average** (they need to work to supplement thier super annuation)
- **4 Are Financially Independant**
- **1 Is Independantly Wealthy**

take that the wrong way, for some of us there was never any *other* way explained or shown to us.

This is all part of the ugly truth and no, this is not some conspiracy theory. In part it has been created by poor management, and in part ignorance.

Let's look at the poor management part shall we?

This was set up long before you or I walked this mortal coil. We could go back to the dawn of civilisation to see where this phenomenon began. It may not even be clear then. However somewhere in our timeline of existence we decided to give our power away (well some did).

People forgot that they were *truly* powerful. They were subjected to a specific way of life; they were told (and some believed, many *still* do) that this was the only way they the world and civilisation could evolve.

That they must subordinate their own wants and desires for the sake of their tribe, country, religion, whatever way you like to put it. And if they did that then they would be looked after, whether that be by being immortalised (which seldom happened), being offered many riches in the afterlife, being told that you will receive a benefit after you retire for your service to the country. You know, all of those sorts of things.

To do this there was a system created, in the early days it was the denial of education to all but the upper echelon of people, let's call them the aristocracy, for lack of a better term.

As we began to evolve as a society education become more important as jobs now required specialist training, there were things that needed a higher level of learning to be able to complete the task at hand (quite often the jobs that the aristocracy did not wish to do themselves).

So now that education was beginning to be a part of everyday life, and that it was available to lower socio economic groups, the aristocracy required a way to control the masses, I mean could you think of what might happen if one of the poorer people in the care of the upper echelon gained knowledge that would help them succeed? They may become more powerful than the people in charge, the people with the money.

The Ugly Truth

And if you think that is absurd, cast your mind back to the early 1900's there was a soldier in the first world war, he made the rank of corporal and was awarded for his bravery. By all accounts this soldier was in fact a high school dropout, and in fact was seen as 'unfit' by his native country of Austria to be enlisted into the army, so he went across the border into Germany and at the outbreak of world war one he enlisted in the German army.

This was an uneducated man, in other words he had not been influenced by the education system, and he was able to effectively take over a country and cause the second world war, in case you are still unsure of who I am referring too it is in fact Adolf Hitler.

I use this only to highlight the issue around education. If we were to look at the ten richest men in the world today, by today's standards 80% of them are 'uneducated', so again not swayed by the system.

There was a system put in place to effectively control the way in which people *think*. There is a programming that has been passed down from generation to generation from hard working and totally loving parents (this is a little about the ignorance part, however I will get to that), products of the 'system'. It is important to note here that this is NOT an attack on systems in general.

Let us now then, have a look at the system. No matter where you look, if you are looking at something that is working perfectly there is some sort of system; heck even if it is not working *perfectly* there may be a system.

Look at the body, we have a circulatory system, without it there would be no way for blood to move around our body taking much needed oxygen to our muscles and brain therefore rendering them useless and lifeless.

So then with that understanding we know we can see that for a nation or city or village, to work then there must be some sort of system. Whether that is a hierarchal system or a democratic system of governance, there is some sort of order.

One of the ways in which this is achieved is through education, or rather the education *'system'*. There is a set curriculum. A lot of what we are taught at school is totally irrelevant to working in the outside world, unless it is a specialist field, and almost all (read all) of it is totally irrelevant to creating wealth and becoming financially independent.

Look around, there are a lot of broke lawyers and doctors (due largely to the wealth paradox).

This is not to say that I am against education, far from it. I value what I learned at school, and I certainly have a lot of time for the teachers that go there to teach.

In fact I have spoken with teachers who are as disillusioned with the curriculum as I am. What I am saying is that there are things that are left out of the curriculum on purpose to effectively create drones. Workers, who will go out and work, pay their taxes and subscribe to the belief that the

The Ugly Truth

government will support them when they hit the retirement age, all of this without question.

If you are having trouble processing that I will give you a minute, sure take a couple to re-read that. When you look back, actually think about what I have just told you here. Look and see if you can see that for yourself, if you are unable then this may not be the book for you.

Yes the government need you to be a drone. If you weren't there to pay your tax, or heaven forbid that you worked out how to manage your money efficiently so as to pay the least amount of tax possible, the country would go broke. Now had the country been run effectively in the first place (like a going concern) then where would be no need for tax, as discussed in the first chapter. It is not in the interest of the (short-sighted) government to provide you with the education that you are able to effectively write your own ticket, instead that is reserved for the people who can afford to go and pay for the even higher education to find that stuff out (or have the nouse to find where it is a seek it out).

This could be the very same people (and in most cases is) who didn't listen or conform to the system to start with. While there are people about who are *unwilling* to take responsibility for where they are in life, then I am afraid this is in fact the way that the government *must* act.

While there are people standing with their hands out playing the victim, there is not a lot that can be done. This is not to say that I think that welfare should be, or even could be, totally abolished.

I think that when there is a real hardship that there should be support. I know from my own experience that it has helped me on occasion, and that should be available to people who really need it.

I like the scene in *'Cinderella Man'* staring Russell Crow, set in the depression. Crowe plays a down on his luck father who is handy with his fists, not wanting charity from anyone or anything, he reluctantly accepts money from a bread line. When he begins to win money by fighting in the squared circle, he goes and repays all that he has *'borrowed'* from welfare. If only society did this, then there would be MUCH more to go round for people.

So the system creates the drones. *What* then, creates the ignorance and cynicism? Realistically, that it is a whole book in itself, so I will try and break it down in a way that is both fun and concise.

I mentioned a little earlier in the chapter about programming being passed down from generation to generation. I can think of a story that was told by Zig Ziglar (and he may have got it from somewhere else), who was a motivational speaker and sales trainer from the United States. Someone whom I hold in high regard and has taught me a great deal.

His wife was cooking a ham, and she cut off the end of the ham, Zig asked her,

"Honey, why did you cut the end off the ham?"

To which she replied,

"I don't know, I have always cut the end off the ham because Mum used to"

Given that her mother was still alive Zig said he had to get to the bottom of it, so he called her and asked her why it was that she cut the end off the ham. The only reason that the end got cut off the ham was so that it would fit in her oven.

You can see by this example that we do things without thinking about it, without questioning it, without a real understanding as to why.

I am sure that if you take stock on your own life and experiences that if you look back you will be able to find similar examples of your own, I know that I can. This is not to say that it is wrong or right, it is merely to highlight that we take these things on without even *thinking* about it or realising.

This can be as simple as something that you hear time after time, it may be from a teacher at school, it may be from your friends, heck there is a good chance that it is from your parents. Ask yourself, did you ever hear your parents say something like *'money doesn't grow on trees?'*

Or what about, *'an apple a day keeps the doctor away'*, You know an apple doesn't hold any magic right?

You know that it is more the belief in that phrase that does anything, and that is *programming*.

Let me share with you a story, this was when I was at school, somehow I got it into my head that I was not popular at school (clearly I was just misunderstood).

This is a thought or belief I had well before I made it into high school where children seem to get even meaner (I want to add here that children LEARN this behaviour, it is not there inherently).

It's like they develop this whole new vocabulary and use it to make other children's live a misery, some do it joking around, and some actually do it with malice.

Anyway, what I got called at high school was 'pork chop' or 'porky' which was ironic as in high school I actually really came into my own physically and when I look back at photos from high school, in my older years at least, I was a very athletic individual with a great physique, yet I didn't think this of myself. In fact it caused a lot of self-doubt and angst.

This seems like a really random story to be telling you right? It is merely to highlight that programming happens without us even knowing it. We go through day-to-day *stuff* and it all builds on top of the layer before.

Before long we actually relate to all of that *stuff* like it is the gospel truth, like there is no way it can be wrong. In short we begin living into that future before it has even arrived.

We become resigned to the fact that there could not *possibly* be another way. I recall having a conversation with my father, for whom I have the utmost admiration and respect.

He and my mother did all they ever could to make sure that we did not go without, (we were loved, respected, supported encouraged, they fed and clothed us, took us all around the country racing BMX) and there is NOTHING more you can ask of your parents, the conversation was in the area of wealth and money.

I basically had said (I was totally resigned and definitely *cynical*)

"The only way I am ever going to be rich is to win lotto"

To which he casually replied,

"Yeah I know what you mean, that is about the only way I am ever going to be rich".

What a totally dis-empowering thing to say, I can feel myself slump just writing it. However that is what I said, and for me at that time, it was *the truth*, the gospel, it was my stuff to hold on to and I was not letting it go.

There, in that moment, in that sentence, in the *language* I was using with myself, it become real for me. That was the future that I was to live into for another 3 years after that.

This is all compounded when we look at the media, the news. Personally I have not watched the news or read a newspaper in a very long time, well at least not in the traditional sense.

People may think that in itself is creating a little ignorance for myself.

I don't see it that way however, and here is why; the media is full of negativity. I could leave it right there and that should be sufficient, yet I feel like I want to share something more with you.

Almost everywhere you look there is a *negative* story.

I'm not saying that some of what is being reported isn't happening, I am simply saying that if there is a story of something that can provide some positive influence to people, some reassurance, then it is often left out of the news, or at the very most given ten seconds of coverage.

Again if you were to look at this yourself and be totally honest then you would see this to be true. So no I don't watch the news or read newspapers, if there is something that is going to directly affect me, or anyone I know, love and care for, the news will find me.

This has proven itself to be true on more than one occasion. I was once in the Military, not sure if I have mentioned it or not... anyway there is a saying (in NZ anyway) that once you are in the services, you never really leave, regardless of whether or not you resign. I certainly relate to this.

I left the military in 2005, and I still have great friends there and great memories, I still feel as though it is part of me.

In 2010 on the 25th of April, I was just finishing breakfast after the ANZAC service on the Gold Coast, with another ex-serviceman from NZ, and we got the news, 3 Squadron of the Royal New Zealand Air Force had lost an Iroquois helicopter and three of the four crew on board.

I did NOT get that news through the paper, or the radio, or the television, I got that news through social media and I was not looking for it, it found me.

So as I have stated here, the news found me. I don't need to read the paper or watch the news that is largely controlled by the governance (or more accurately a very wealthy family), if it is relevant to me, the news will find me.

This chapter, although it might look that way, is not about bashing the powers that be, it is not about sticking it to the man. It is more about letting you know that the system is not designed to spit out or create people who are capable of becoming independently wealthy.

As stated, it is about the understanding that the aristocracies are content with creating drones that will do what they are told and not question why. Luckily we live (well a good proportion of us anyway) in a country where we are able to make that choice for ourselves, and actually change the outcome. We do not have to be a slave to that mandate, we are able to learn these new approaches, and hopefully pass them on to our children so that they can do the same. This is how we get on top of the ignorance around wealth creation and money.

I wish that I could say that was the worst of it all, however unfortunately it is not. There is a flaw in the system, and that is that it creates an unsustainable model.

As the older generation leave the work force, they are not being replaced, in a lot of cases, they are being replaced by machines or programs.

There are two reasons for this, one being that they simply cannot fill that position or the company simply found a more efficient way of doing business. In both cases it means there is less tax revenue coming into the government of the time.

This means that they either have to put taxes up, or bring welfare down. This is a very broad over view of and in no way should be considered as the only outcome, this is my view of it, and of how it occurs to me. It is based upon other cultures and societies that have gone before us.

So the *ugly truth* is this, the government in its current form will not be able to sustain a welfare system that will provide you with any sort of lifestyle what so ever.

If we looked at it today the benefit received from an average couple on the pension does little, if anything, to cover the everyday expenses of life.

And this is all on the assumption that you are in perfect health, so add that in to the mix also, assume that you have your own home, you will have rates to pay that will increase every year with inflation, where your pension will more than likely decrease.

OK so you don't have your own house, you rent... so once your rent is paid then you have nothing left of your pension to buy groceries.

If you think I am being a little dramatic I invite you to do the investigation yourself, it is not pretty.

I am telling you this, as I truly believe that we all have the *ability* and *right* to create our own outcome, our own reality.

If you want to scrape by on the scraps from the government then absolutely, put your head in the sand and pray that it will all be OK, on the other hand if you want something more from life then stand up and be counted.

Throughout the series that follows this book you will have the opportunity and ability to create new income streams that will not only provide you with the material things and possessions that you want, it will also provide you with much more than that, it will provide you with a vehicle that you can provide the sort of education for your children that no government or aristocracy could provide.

The big thing that it will provide for you is choice, or more to the point freedom of choice in the things that you really wish to experience.

Don't fall for the lies that are doled out from the leaders of your country, make your own choices, the ugly truth does not have to be your ugly truth.

TYPES OF INCOME

"Money never starts an idea. It is always the idea that starts the money"
~Owen Laughlin

It would be a good idea to mention the types of income that are out there, it would be logical right? I mean this is a book about creating the foundations for *multiple streams of income* after all.

There are basically two types of income when you break it down, *Passive* income and *Active* income. The latter is in essence a J.O.B. and if you are wondering about the acronym for J.O.B. it stands for *Just Over Broke*, as with one of those things that is all you are ever going to be. This is essentially where you are trading time for money.

They can be handy for getting a start, however they should not be considered as a long-term solution. In fact if you asked my opinion they should be a little like training wheels, and be taken off when competent to live on your own.

I realise that this in itself creates other issues, so this is more than likely why the majority have *jobs*, which is fine, means there is a bigger slice of the pie for those who are willing to go out and get some.

I am not saying that if you truly love your JOB that you should give it up, if you are happy stay there, there is no harm in that, I am saying that if you want any sort of *retirement* or freedom that you should very well consider the fact that you are going to need more than one income source, and most certainly one that works *without* you.

I want to break down and qualify these two types of income that I am referring too.

Our *ultimate* goal through creating multiple streams of income is to create streams that work *independently* of us, therefore creating residual (on going) *passive* income.

Let us have a quick look at the types of passive income.

I would like to ask a question, have you ever heard of a guy by the name of Elvis Presley? What about John Lennon, or perhaps Michael Jackson? What do all of these people have in common?

Sure they were all musicians, artists of entertainment. But there is something else they have in common and I am wondering if by now you have figured it out? Let me shed some light on it, just in case you are still in the dark on what I am digging at.

It is this, they are all dead and *still making millions of dollars every year*. But how can that be? I mean if you were to die, would your pay cheque stop coming in? If you are gainfully employed, you bet your bottom dollar it would, sure you might have life insurance and your family may get some monetary consideration, but that will only go so far.

Elvis has been dead since 1977, at the time of writing this a good 37 years, and yet there is still money coming into his estate. So again I ask, how can this be?

Well it is the darnedest thing; the income that he receives all these years after his death is *royalty* income. Every musician who has had an album released can say they receive it too; well at least they can *if* their album sells and gets airplay.

Musicians are not the only ones of course that can create this royalty type of income. Actors, Authors, photographers, artists, basically anyone who in effect licenses out the use of their intellectual property (IP), trademarks, copyrights or patents.

So yes, if you invented something that people could not live without and then had the presence of mind to trade mark it or better yet have a patent on that something, then you could license out the production and distribution of it and simply collect a fee for the privilege of someone else using your idea. Brilliant!

Now why didn't I think of that? Wait I have, you can buy my album on iTunes, just search for *'Drew Hawkes, Scattered Thoughts'*.

When we look at the dictionary definition of royalty it says this;

Royalty: A sum of money paid to a patentee for the use of a patent or to an author or composer for each copy of a book sold or for each public performance of a work.

So if we were to simplify the definition of royalty income, we could say: *'do the work once, get paid for life'*. That works for me just fine.

I am sure you can see the merit in that right? You don't have to be an inventor, you don't have to be a musician, or really any of the things that have been suggested to create this *type* of income.

If we really looked hard at royalty income, we can see that it is passive, once the initial work is done, there is really not a lot of input from us, if any at all, for us to continue to receive dividends or income from it.

So if we look at it from that stand point, what are some of the things that you could consider to be an opportunity in your own life where you could create a passive income flow?

I am sure that you have some knowledge that you have gained over the years, and I can guarantee that someone out there would find that information extremely valuable right?

Let me give you an example, you purchased this book presumably because you wanted the information contained within the pages to learn how to create and sustain multiple income streams. Now let me ask a further question, did you pay for it? (It's not a trick question).

This is work that I have done once, yet every time someone buys this book, I get paid.

So maybe you don't want to write and publish a book, that is fine. What I am getting at is that you have some great information in your head that I know people would pay for. You would not believe some of the crazy niches that are out there that people are making money in, seriously.

So you don't want to write. Can you talk? If you can talk, you can create a product where you do the work once and people will continue to pay you for years to come. From that you can even have someone transcribe your audio and create an eBook for you, and now you have two products, or at the very least a more valuable one.

Look I am getting a little off track here so let me bring it back, I will touch more on the products and your information a little later in the book, for now let us get back to the types of income.

So still on the passive side of things, other examples of passive income can be in the form of businesses that you invest in, investing in the stock market, renting property. You may argue that some of what was just mentioned is not *really* passive income as there is an amount of work that you must do in order for them to work. To which I would say that it very much depends on how you have them set up, as with anything. I mean you still must do the work at some stage, if you do it smartly enough however, you can do it once and get paid for ever.

Does this all make sense to you? Good. The thing with humans, as a species, is that we seriously love to over complicate things and really make it all a bit hard. I am no different to the next person in that respect, fortunately for me, now, I am able to see when I am doing this and stop before I make the very possible totally impossible (because I really think we do that far too much).

I think it is pertinent to mention here that winning lotto or some sort of lottery is NOT passive income, it is simply gambling, and it is by no means going to provide you security… unless of course you have won over two million dollars and have that money *invested* in a high interest account. Even then it could be more trouble than it is worth.

On a side note there, of all of the people who have actually won the lottery, over 70% of them will lose it all, in fact of that 70% and even higher percentage will be worse off than they were... why is that I wonder?

So *passive income* therefore, is an income that continues to come in month in month out, without you having to go out and 'work' for it.

It is, as I have said here in this chapter, if there is somewhere that you can do the work once and get paid forever with minimal, if any, input from yourself. That is passive. Books, Music, Patents, eBooks, Audios and even online or offline home study courses, they are all examples of things that can bring you passive income.

That then leaves the other type of income, which of course is *Active*.

Now if passive is something that is coming in from work we have done once and do not necessarily have to do again... what do you think that Active income might be? It's kind of a loaded question right?

Of course it is income that you are going to have to go out and continue to work for, a simple time for money trade. Now again, I would like to point out here, that although I personally do not like this type of income, I understand that sometimes it can be *perceived* as a necessary evil in order to get you from where you are now, to where you want to indeed head.

And if you are in a position that you truly love, and you would do it even if you were not getting monetarily rewarded for it then I would say, good for you keep it up.

If however on the other hand you are doing it out of some sort of misplaced *'sense of duty'* to someone else then get your head out of your arse and start doing something that is going to make you happy. You only get one shot at this life, and all you ever have, all you can ever be sure of, is the *moment* that you are in right now… and now...

The past is the past, it does not exist but in the mind of the person *thinking* about it, and the future is an illusion. All that there is, is RIGHT NOW. If you are having trouble processing what you have just read, that is ok, you are allowed to, read it again to see if you can get some more from it.

If you want more on that, then read *The Power of Now, Ekhart Tolle.* If you are toiling away at some JOB that you despise in that hope that 'one day' you will be able to truly live the life you want to live, then get a grip.

Stop, THINK, and take action NOW in the order of the thing that you want to achieve in life, no one is going to do it for you, and no one is going to die if you actually do something for yourself, and become that which you are meant to be.

Active income can be OK to pay the day to day bills, however it should never be seen as the way in which you are going to be able to create a long term and secure future for yourself and your family, and to think that way is not only futile, it is more than a little naive also.

Now for many people what you have just read will be something that is kind of hard to take in and work through. I would like you to consider that is because society has been teaching us to think a totally different way for a very long time.

As mentioned in previous chapters, it is not in the aristocracy's interest to have the masses be financially literate, if it was there would be financial literacy taught in schools.

I know that people need money to pay for day to day necessities, and I know that it can be a challenge in altering your mind in order to take advantage of a totally abundant universe, I know this, as I myself had these struggles, as have many self-made success stories.

I am sure you have read or heard about them right? However it must be said that the success came to these people, and myself, *after* we removed ourselves from the illusion of security that was offered in a JOB. And unfortunately that is all that it is, and illusion.

Look, you may very well be saying 'hey Andrew, if everyone thought the way that you are telling them to think, then there would be no one to carry out the day to day tasks of society, like pumping gas, fixing toilets and drainage, building houses, selling groceries, and so on and so forth, and perhaps you are right…

However I am not talking to them, I am talking to *you*, and if someone lent you this book to read it is because they think enough about you and *respect you enough* to share this amazing gift of mindset with you.

Sure if everyone thought this way, then maybe there would be no one to do those jobs, history would show us that the likely hood of everyone thinking this way are very slim, so there is always going to be someone there to do those jobs... that said, it does *not* have to be you.

You have a choice.

Making the shift from active income worker to passive income life-styler does not have to be a difficult one.

Given that what I have just told you is a lot to take in, well certainly if you have never thought that way, then we are going to need to provide a bridge of sorts for you to be able to go out and make this happen, you are going to need something that is going to provide you with some proof and a little confidence to get you started.

It need not be expensive for you to start to grow a passive income. Look not at the numbers, look instead at the percentages. I guarantee this will blow your mind.

I once had a friend in primary school, we used to do heaps together, in fact we both went for the lead in our school play, we could both sing, however I pipped him for the role... fast forward 20 odd years and I looked him up on Facebook (as you do) and managed to make contact.

I thought it would be pretty cool to catch up... we didn't really talk much, anyway one day I posted a status saying, what if you could turn a one-time investment of $25 into 22k a month? (Seldom do these payout for the average person) to which he wrote a scathing reply... all I did was ask a question... however the response I got was from a supposed financial advisor, ok so look at the percentages, it's about a 9000% return per month, so yes pretty huge, and for most unbelievable...

I am not going to tell you that I made that work to that extent, however I am going to share with you that same opportunity I invested 25$ once and now get a 350% return each and every month... again not that the money is a lot, however the percentage is something that is all too often scoffed at and simply dismissed as unobtainable. When the truth of the matter is, people are simply too scared to act.

And the biggest reason they are too scared to act is simply because society has made them that way. I am not giving anyone an out here as *we* are all *responsible* for our *lot* in life, you do what you do.

Yet society has given people an easy out by creating this myth that only the *special* people can have this sort of success of return. If I had a dollar for every time that I have heard someone (who has not actually tasted financial success) say that if something is too good to be true then it probably is, I could retire on interest alone, what a complete and utter fucking cop out.

People only say that because they are too scared to try something for fear that they might not look so good to their *friends* if they were to *fail*.

To all those people I say good luck, as mentioned earlier, there is going to be no one to look after them, the current, so called, social welfare system of most developed countries is totally unsustainable.

Unless they take this on board, and take it very seriously, then they will be literally left out in the cold. What we are witnessing now (at the time of first print, relative time 2008-2013 and beyond) is really just the beginning. Over time there has been empires come and go, and if people think that it will not, or cannot happen again, then they are clearly living in a state of delirium (and I am not talking about excitement).

OK, then how would you dip your toe in? Simple, find a low entry affiliate or networking company, there are plenty out there, the one I mentioned above is GDI, they sell domain names, and get started.

Share it with your friends, help them share it, gift them a copy of this book if you're worried about offending them and don't want to tell them to take their head out of their butt and get going. What are you waiting for?

Remember what you read earlier, we are on the cusp of the Greatest Wealth Transfer in the History of Mankind, there will be no prizes for second, however there are massive rewards in helping others get this information you now have, and helping them to use it and make a difference. It only takes one person (at a time) to stand up and be brave, if not you then it may well be the next person and you may miss out.

Something I want to add to this. It is something that Tim Ferriss talks about in 'The Four Hour Work Week'. It is a concept of *relative Income v's Absolute income.*

We're taught that a person who receives $100,000pa (person A) as a salary is better off, or wealthier than a person who receives say $60,000pa (person B). On the face of it, that is true.

If however we through in some other *variables* the context changes. Here is what I mean.

Let's assume that person A works 80 hours a week for that $100,000 his hourly rate is $26, this is based on a 48 week working year, person A gets four weeks for his hard work.

Now look at person B works 20 hours a week (at a stretch) and has the free time to work on the things he/she is passionate about. Working s full 52 weeks (person B can take time when they please) Person B's hourly rate works out to be $57.

Person A has an *absolute* income, person B has a *relative* income. Person A has an income that is based on whether or not they turn up at work and the amount of time they put in, it is a trade of time for money. Person B can scale his/her income by simply increasing certain aspects of his/her output and is not trading time for money. (this is in its most basic form, read Tim's book for more information)

MULTIPLE INCOME STREAMS

"It's a tough business if you don't know what you are doing. But it can be extremely lucrative and rewarding when you learn the ropes."
~Robert G. Allen

So there was this guy once, his father was a school teacher. Once he left school he enlisted in the Merchant Navy and then transferred to the Marines as a Gunship Pilot in Vietnam.

He did his service, left the military and started working for Xerox selling copiers; he rose to be the top sales man for the company before starting out on his own with a Velcro Surfer Wallet business. This was a business that would teach him much of what he needed to know in order to ultimately succeed.

What he failed to do with that business was secure the *intellectual property*, which then enabled people to copy the idea, market it much better, and reduce the manufacturing cost, effectively putting him out of business, owing just over $700,000 to creditors, which he repaid within a 12 month period.

In case you are unsure of whom I am referring too, I am of course talking about Robert Kiyosaki. Author, real estate investor and entrepreneur.

Robert has now published over 15 different titles on entrepreneurship, investing, and building businesses. Many successful people have attributed their success to strategies and ideas they gained by reading many of his titles. The reason that I bring him up is to highlight a few things about income streams and also to go over a couple of his philosophies, one in particular.

In 1996-97 (this is hazy as 'Rich Dad, Poor Dad' was written to launch and market the game), Robert Released a Game Called 'Cashflow 101' which basically taught financial literacy with regards to basic stock investment, property investment, and business investments in a safe environment, it was safe and risk free due to the fact that it is played with play money.

It educates the players in different financial strategies and scenarios where the player can generate new *'passive income'* to enable themselves to leave the 'rat race'. The premise for the game is pretty simple, there are two parts to the game, the first to *escape the rat race*, and the second (which is called the fast track), to ultimately win the game, is to generate an additional $50,000 per month in income ($50,000 more than you entered the fast track with) or to invest into your dream, which ever happens first.

In essence, the game is only hard, or difficult, *until you have left the 'rat race'* and then it becomes much easier, it is a classic take on life itself and clearly highlights that becoming wealthy is not *dependent* on the amount of income you have from a J.O.B.

The players are given chances to invest their income into different ventures, this is to provide an education on the different vehicles that are available and how it can be done, but moreover to stimulate the brain into considering, or entertaining if you like, the fact that it can be achieved in real life.

The reason I wanted to bring this up, was to highlight the basic fundamental, that Kiyosaki so eloquently displays with this game, and that is simply when you have enough passive income to support your lifestyle, you know, pay your bills etc. without the need to trade time for money, i.e. have more money coming in than is going out regardless of what activity you are doing, then you have real choices and freedom. Do you follow?

It could not be made any simpler than that, and at the end of the day this is 100% true, no matter where you are in the world, no matter what your religious or political views are and regardless of whether or not it is night or day.

If it is this simple then, why the heck is not everyone doing this?

Well the short answer is because most people are lazy. Yeah I think I may have mentioned it, if not, it is the truth.

I don't mean they have no work ethic, as there are many people that do. I mean that they are too lazy to think. Henry Ford said it perfectly when he said;

"Thinking is the hardest work there is, which is probably the reason so few engage in it".
~Henry Ford

This could be in part due to the fact that society have conditioned them to be this way, it could simply be that they are unsure where to begin, so then it all gets a little hard, and once it gets hard, they get lethargic and before you know it, 65 years has gone by and they are asking for a hand out in the form of a pension.

Genuinely believing that they deserve to get one, and maybe 100 years ago they did, unfortunately the writing has been on the wall for a long time that the status quo was unsustainable (as mentioned previously) and still people choose to bury their heads in the sand.

Let's lighten it up a little, so with this super simple information in mind (its ok we will break it down further) you can now start to map out what it would take to 'retire'.

Now retirement to me does not mean giving up work and playing golf or fishing every day, although if you wanted to do that then, by all means, *you could.*

No retirement to me is simply being able to have the choice to do what I want to do on any given day, to have the resources available that I am able to do the things I love and enjoy, travel, invest, travel, dine out, travel, fishing, hunting, *travel.*

It would mean doing the things that were *important to you*, if that was volunteering at a hostel, reading to the blind, ending world hunger, whatever it is.

By exiting the *'rat race'* then you are able to focus on what is important without having to worry about where the next pay cheque is coming from. So you set up *multiple income streams* right?

In case this is still not making sense to you let's have a little look at 'life' (well most peoples anyway).

For the sake of this example let us assume that we have left school and are educated (at least to high school anyway, as that is about as far as I went).

Right, so we have left school and we have got ourselves a J.O.B. (which remember stands for Just Over Broke) we start getting some money in, we now have a little more freedom than perhaps we did when we had our paper round or did odd jobs around the neighborhood to get 'pocket money'.

Less than 10% of us save anything from that time, most of it gets spent on partying, new toys, buying gadgets, you get the picture right?

We then might look at getting a property, because that is what our parents taught us to do (in most cases), or because it is the 'done thing'. Only we get it wrong, we buy a property and *live in it*, no financial advantage in that.

In fact now it is a liability, it is costing you each and every month, but it was the right thing to do, think of 35 years' time when it is all paid off (***cough*** ha-ha, yeah right!).

The bank, due to your *outstanding payment history* offer you a new credit card with a 20k limit, its ok though as they can just add it to your home loan, it's all secure, no problems.

Only now you are *stuck*… each and every month you have to make those repayments, if you don't then the bank will take your house. (BTW, just so you know, the bank does not want to take your house as it makes them look incompetent and blemishes their lending record and credit rating.

OK, so back to being trapped, when you are in this cycle, you are in fact like a rat on a treadmill, you are going nowhere, you must take different action to have a different result.

"Insanity - doing the same thing over and over expecting a different result"
~ Albert Einstein

You go to work, as do most, and you earn your money. You get your money, less what the government takes in tax, the bills come in, the money goes out, and with whatever is left you try to have a life.

There really is never enough money to cover the month. The worst part is that you never seem to get ahead of the curve, I mean you start earning more money and it still does not cover what is going out.

That, ladies and gents, is what is referred to as the *'Wealth Paradox'*, however I am going to touch on that a little later.

The thing that wealthy people, or more accurately, *financially literate* people, do with their money is this - they earn it, pay for what they need, invest some of it and pay tax on what is left over, usually a lot less than the average person.

This a VERY broad over view on all of that, if you want more depth then by all means read the book *'Rich Dad, Poor Dad' by Robert Kiyosaki*, it gives a pretty good explanation of the concept.

All the while you *want* to have more out of life, you see other people having it, yet you can't seem to make that money stretch that far. How do they do it?

Simple, they create new streams of income. I don't know of many people who have retired independently wealthy (in fact I personally don't know any), who have done so solely on their wage of 45 years and savings.

It may have been done, however I would say that they would be the exception to the rule.

So, if they're creating new streams of income, *how* do they do it? They either have something that they recognise in themselves that has inherent value to someone and leverage that, or they find out where they can get education on a particular wealth creation vehicle and then learn to drive it.

This does NOT need to take up a huge amount of time... let me say that again, this does NOT need to take up a huge amount of time.

This chapter was not intended to be a lecture, it was more over intended to show the importance of, and *why* you would set up multiple income streams. When you break it down it is this simple equation, that when mastered and understood, will provide you with the lifestyle and freedom that few people ever truly get to realise, and I would have to say that is because they don't see how simple this should be, and in fact is.

When the passive income stream (money you have either done the work once for that will pay you forever, or money that you no longer have to work for) is greater than the outgoings then you have the freedom of choice.

I have said right in this chapter that you are stuck… so *how to get unstuck?*

The first thing I would suggest is educating yourself, and given the fact that you are in fact reading this, I have said it before, however you really do deserve to hear it again, you *are already ahead of the game*. At the end of this book there are going to be some ways in which to raise some capital in order for you to get a start, for now it is important that you are thinking about new income streams and understand the fact that without them you are going nowhere fast.

Near the start of this chapter I mentioned that I wanted to look a little closer into a couple of Kiyosaki's philosophies, so we'll delve into that now.

In *'The Cashflow Quadrant'*, Robert Kiyosaki talks about the four parts of the quadrant. They are;

E, for the Employee, where most of the world's population hang out, paying the highest in taxes to governments.

S, for Self Employed, these people still end up paying more in tax than they need to, and are really people who have brought themselves a job (we will expand on this).

B, which is Business owners, now in the book Kiyosaki defines business as having more than 500 employees (also something we will go into more a bit later). And last but not least,

I, which stands for investor and would be the ultimate goal for creating true passive income.

This book is really more about the second two rather than the first, however from the second of the first, the S quadrant.

You can in fact graduate that into the second two, and the secret is in not being, or rather working, in the business, but working on it.

I am sure you would have heard that before, and as stated above it is something we will go deeper into, first though I wanted to touch on the B quadrant.

With techniques and strategies for running businesses with the advances in technology that we have had, it is very possible for you to be in business with you being the only employee of your company.

I will explain what I mean, however I will add this caveat, to get a deeper understanding of what we are going to discuss now, and how it pertains to the B quadrant, read the afore mentioned book by Robert Kiyosaki.

No longer are we bound by geographical location, with the internet and advances in communication portals, like *Skype* and *Facetime*, it has become easier to find competent people to help you run your business. Whether that is through having a virtual PA, or having an outbound call centre to generate leads for your business.

For most businesses there is at least one thing that can be handled by someone off site (or even off shore for that matter).

There are at least a half dozen sites on the internet where people (free lancers) will bid for your work, now of course the onus is still on you to make sure that you hire, or contract, the right person for the job or project and get value for money, however you can get good quality people to do the work for literally pennies in the dollar.

This is not because you are taking advantage of them, in fact in most cases, the money that you agree on for any given project, would be a lot more than they would normally receive, it is because there is a lot of competition out there for work, remember that there are hard times for people.

So what would be an example of what you could get these 'contractors' to do for you? Well, a good portion of marketing your business online is creating back links to your website, one of the ways in which this can be achieved is by writing a number of articles related to your business field providing *information that would be useful to the reader*.

So you could find yourself someone at one of these sites to write articles for you. You could make it a simple one-time project, or you could make it on going. You agree, in advance, on a reasonable price for the project, you create the guidelines for what your articles should cover and ask to see them before they are published.

You may say that this is a simple task, and to be fair it is, however can you yourself write an article for $2? And before you jump in an say, *"yes I can, in fact it costs me nothing when I write it"*, consider that it might take you an hour to write an article to publish, what could you do with that hour if you invested in your business, and what is that hour worth, even if you are only earning $15 an hour, then you are still $13 an hour better off if you have someone else do it and pay them $2. You follow?

You could also find someone to take care of graphic work for your company, or project, perhaps you have a great idea and have a lot of research that you have accumulated however you don't have the time to create an information product from it, you could find someone and have them put create a product from it.

Keep in mind that you are not doing this because you are lazy, you are doing it as you understand the *value of your time* and can more than likely put it to better use in other areas of your business.

You can have them conduct research or find answers to specific questions that you need to be able to create a product from it. There are so many ways in which you can utilize such a service.

The point I am making here is that no longer do you need to have 500 employees to be big business, you can be your one employee and have contractors to carry out task to grow your business.

There are plenty of advantages in operating your business in this way, you are able to leverage your time more efficiently, it is more economical, and you do not have to manage your workers tax (as they are contracted, not employed).

For example, let's look at one of my previous businesses, The Affordable Website Co, as the name suggests the company built websites at an affordable rate, and yes I can build websites, I just don't anymore, my time is better invested in other areas of my business. I was the only employee of that company however I had 8 other people working for me, this is a number that was easily scalable if needed, and the people who were there, were selected with the future in mind, i.e. they were capable of hiring and managing other contractors that came on board with the company as work load and demand increased, as they are contractors they are paid only for the work they did.

This is not new of course, however most people don't consider it for traditional business, and they should, there are huge economic and financial benefits in conducting your business this way (I am not an accountant, and this is NOT financial advice, please discuss the best option for you with your accountant).

By having these people 'working' for me, it then frees me up to expand my businesses or write books, spend more time with family and invest my money in other ventures so that it works for me and develop new and exciting income streams.

It basically gives me time freedom (forget the money for now) to be able to work on the things that I enjoy doing, and it has been very well documented, that if you are doing something you enjoy then you are much more likely to succeed with it.

Sure there is some management that comes into play there, however we ALL have that in us, if true financial independence is what you want, then you have to remove yourself from the machine to work on it (you want to make sure you have great systems in place to do this with the best results).

With the management, then you basically oversee what is happening, once the income stream that you are working on is at a point where there is a decent return on it, then train someone to manage it for you, then you can get paid simply for having the nous to set it up correctly to begin with.

For tips on the best way to set your business up so that is has the best chance of success of working independently of you then I highly recommend reading *'The E-Myth' by Michael Gerber*, I would say to any business owner or would be entrepreneur that this is mandatory reading. To provide another working example of what I am referring to, I want to reference *'The Four Hour Workweek' by Timothy*

Ferriss, in this book, Tim highlights some of the best ways in which you are able to outsource your business tasks and take 'mini retirements'.

In the book Tim mentions that his company has only one employee, however the size of the organization is well over 200 people, pretty close to big business, as Robert Kiyosaki would look at it.

I know that this book, and particularly this chapter, is about the importance creating multiple income streams, however I wanted to include that just to show you that is need not be a daunting thing, you can grow a pretty decent size organization without a huge capital outlay (make sure you set it up right to begin with), or simply outsource the things that you don't like to do (those that can be outsourced of course).

So by now you should well know that I am a fan of having more than one income stream, and the importance of why you will want to set them up, so with that in mind, I think it time that we look at an income stream that you yourself can look at implementing, you will be able to use some of what we have talked about here to help generate income faster and to a point where you can then use the money you generate from that to build even bigger and better businesses.

Before we dive into that though, and I know you are dying to get into it, I want you to first complete an exercise. You may very well have done this before, then again it may be a totally new experience for you and quite revealing.

I want you to imagine what it is that you want to experience in your life, the car you want to drive, the home you want to live in, do you want to have a live-in chef? How about a nanny for your children?

Think of how you would like your life to be. Make the list resemble how you would like to live your life day to day if there were no limits. It might look something like this.

I drive an Audi Q7 with all the options, I live in a six-room designer home on the water's edge, and we have a 45' boat moored on our private jetty. Most nights we have dinner waiting for us that is cooked by our resident chef, who also looks after the house. Every week we have a masseuse come to our home to give both my wife and I massages and a personal trainer that comes every other day.

OK, so there is a quick example of what I mean when I say what you would like your life to be, you can even add in the holidays that you would like to take, the reason being we are going to break each one down and give it a value, or cost.

For example we'll say that an Audi Q7 fully optioned sells for $220,000.00 finance at 7% over 4 years would mean that the repayments are $4,400 with a balloon payment of $44,000 (which you could have the option of rolling into a new car). The six room home on the water might be $10,000 a month, the boat, again, let's says its financed, $450,000 at 12% over 4 years, would be about $12,000 per month, we'll say that our chef gets paid 60,000 a year (as we provide him/her with lodgings) so that is $5,000 a month, a masseuse, say $1,000 a month, groceries and living expenses, let's call them $6,000 a month. Now we add them up (per month expense).

$4,400 car

$10,000 House

$12,000 Boat

$5,000 Chief

$1,000 Masseuse

$6,000 Living

$38,400 Total Monthly Expenses

OK, so you don't *need* to be obnoxious about it, I am simply illustrating a point, now that we know what our monthly expenses are, all we need to do is to generate that sort of income and we are free.

There is likely a voice in your head telling you that this is not possible, I would like you to consider this is perhaps the exact reason you have not yet done it.

Look this was, as I said, to illustrate a point, you don't have to use big figures like that, it could very well be that all you need each and every month to be free is to generate an extra $5,000. So as stated, we are going to explore some ways in which you can do exactly that, and believe me, once you have worked out how to generate that then you can easily scale it and generate more.

The biggest thing that will hold you back with this, is yourself, your old ways of thinking. Ways of thinking that have not really benefited you in the past. We must be prepared to *suspend disbelief* in order for us to truly soar to our full potential.

With this information in hand, we can now begin on starting some of these income streams, you can add this list to your goals and we can get into generating new income streams.

> *"People become really quite remarkable when they start thinking that they can do things. When they believe in themselves, they have the first secret of success."*
> *~Norman Vincent Peale*

RIVERS OF GOLD

"Adversity has the effect of eliciting talents, which in prosperous circumstances would have lain dormant".
~Horace

Throughout this book I have followed a pretty common theme, and that is one of self-reliance. Although there may be a lot of people that you depend upon, or rely on, there is really only one person that you can be sure will always stand by you no matter way (that is of courses unless you the let the little voice in your head talk you out of shit before you begin) and that one person is you.

I remember going to a seminar in Melbourne Australia, the draw cards for me to go were, *Sir Richard Branson* and *Timothy Ferriss*. Both of whom I have the utmost respect for, Tim went to at least 26 different publishers before one took his idea and said,

"yes, we are going to publish it."

The previous publishers all said that they did not see the merit in it and that it would not sell at all... If you don't know who Timothy Ferriss is, perhaps you have heard of his International Best Seller, *The Four Hour Workweek* (I have mentioned it a couple of times).

What Tim had to rely on was his *own resolve*, even when people (so called experts) told him that it would not work, he pushed-on anyway, he relied on himself. It did help that Tim is fanatical about testing everything, and he already knew that the title was a winner by split testing it against others using Google Pay Per Click network, and he had researched his timing to market to ensure the best possible chance of success.

What I am saying with this is don't always rely on someone else's advice, investigate yourself to ensure your best possible outcome.

If you have not read any of his books I recommend you looking him up and doing just that, you will learn things that will complement what this book will teach you and make life about as easy as it could ever get.

It's important to note here that all of what Tim did to test and measure in the lead-up to publishing his book are in fact, skills that anyone who is serious about succeeding in anything, can learn freely by researching the millions of pages of information available online.

The key there is actually researching; most people (and I have moments myself) are far too lazy to get out of their own way to achieve. You are clearly not included in that statement, after all you are reading, and you are reading a book that is telling you *"You have rivers of gold just waiting to be uncovered"*

Sir Richard Branson needs no introduction, that is of course unless you have been living under a rock for the past 40 odd years...

This is of course someone who relies heavily on not only his own resolve, but his uncanny intuition also. I have heard many people speak from the platform, and to be fair, people that have a far firmer grasp on public speaking than Sir Richard, however when you are in the same Auditorium as Sir Richard, there is an unmistakable presence.

Love him or hate him, you have got to respect what he has achieved. I was totally blown away at the generosity and authenticity of the man, and I feel privileged to have been able to be present to hear what he had to say that night, what made it even more special was the fact that he was wearing an All Black's jersey that was gifted to him by none other than *Knight in waiting*, Richie McCaw.

Being a Kiwi myself, I thought this was pretty cool. This is a man who discovered and uncovered (and still does) many hidden rivers of gold within his own life. He wanted to be an advocate for students, so he created a student magazine, he soon learned that he needed something to fund the magazine, so he started a mail order record company as it was, mainstream music was expensive at the time. This, of course, was just the tip of the iceberg for Sir Richard, yet these are the very examples that one could look at to say;

> "OK, so there was a problem to which he found a solution, what can I learn from that?"

There is an episode of The Simpson's where Homers long lost brother Herb is now living on the street due to Homer ruining his company.

In this episode Herb learns of Homer winning the lottery, all of $200, yet Herb decides that Homer owes it to him for crashing his company. I won't detail the whole episode, yet what I will share with you is this, as it is something I believe is VERY powerful and very relevant to this book.

What Herb says this to Lisa;

> "all anyone needs in this life to be wealthy and make money is simply an idea, and some start-up capital".

And I totally agree with that, however I would suggest to you that start-up capital does not necessarily mean dollars and cents, your start-up capital may be in the form of *sweet equity*, you know doing the yards you can do without putting money up to get your thing happening, and of course the desire to actually make it happen.

There are so many ways in which to get started, in fact when you start looking you get a little overwhelmed with which way is the best way to start. I have proven, to myself and others, time and time again that you don't need dollars and cents to start, and even make a business venture profitable.

Look at what Sir Richard has done, look for the simple things that he did *almost right* and learn what you can. You can check out any of his books from the library, take action and make it happen.

I have said, I was there mainly to see those two people, and to talk with someone else whom I admire and respect Mr Nik Halik, *The Thrillionaire*™, he is Australia's first civilian qualified Astronaut. This is a guy that created a top 10 goal list when he was only a boy of 10 years old, and now at 45 (at the time of writing this book) he has ticked off 8 of the 10, a list that included having lunch on the bow of the Titanic, becoming an astronaut, running with the bulls in Pamplona, summiting the world's highest peaks, becoming a rock star, these are a few of his top ten, why would I tell you this? All of these great activities need to be funded somehow, and Nik become a self-made millionaire in is 20's by taking some of the strategies outlined in this book, and series, and putting them to use.

However when I got there, there were so many great speakers to see I did not know where to start. I saw Timothy Ferriss, I saw Nik speak, and I got content and information that I could use to help myself and to help others also. I guess though the reason that I am telling you that I was there was all of the bonus stuff that I got that was unexpected.

I have long said to my wife that it is always the intangible things that you get so much from at events like this, the contacts you make, the conversations that you have, the little snippets you hear that you might not normally have heard.

This event was hosted by a company called 21st Century Education, a company that has a vision not too dissimilar to mine, in making financial education available to anyone and everyone that is willing to do what it takes, owned by another person who was a self-made millionaire in his 20's, a man by the name of Jamie McIntyre.

It was something that Jamie said in his opening address, or presentation that I want to touch on here and I am including it as it helped me immensely, even now.

When he started on his entrepreneurial journey, he was couch surfing at a friend's place nearly 150k in debt. I will be paraphrasing here a little, it will not be word for word however you will get the picture.

He tracked down a mentor who was prepared to work with him and teach him about a millionaire mindset. That is not such uncommon story (well for many successful people anyway), the next part of Jamie's story is what got me thinking, and that is why I am sharing it here, to hopefully make you THINK. What was said next was that Jamie's mentor told him to make a list of all of his assets and his liabilities, I'm sure you would have done at least one of these yourself, certainly if you have been to any personal development seminar. Jamie basically said to his mentor,

"Well that's easy, I have no assets and I am 150k in debt".

His mentor said;

"No assets? Of course you have assets, anyone of your age (very early 20's) who can get themselves into 150k worth of debt, has assets, you obviously convinced someone to believe in you and lend you the money".

That is the bit you all need to get, *having assets is NOT about having material things*, and in fact in most cases material things are generally liabilities at any rate.

By that I mean, if it something that is producing you income, it is an asset, if it something that is costing you money, or not providing a return, then it is a liability. No, having assets is about more, much more than that.

One of the biggest assets you can have is your mindset, however, this *is* something that needs to be consistently worked on, otherwise it can very quickly turn into a liability.

I am fascinated with Quantum Physics, and if you have had anything at all to do with Quantum Physics you will know what I am talking about when I say that you create your reality by the things you think, the things you say, and the actions you take.

With that in mind, is why I say that your mindset can also very quickly become a liability, you must continually fill your mind with good information, good brain food. Failure to do so will see you fall back into old habits, thinking patterns and conditioning.

With Quantum Physics you either love it or hate it, and most hate it due to the fact that it is kind of hard to get a grip of, it challenges everything that they have always believed to be real.

In fact *this* is quite literally why most people don't try, *it challenges their most closely held beliefs* and often turns them into myth.

If they found out that everything they have ever believed in was not real, they would have nothing to defend or believe in. This is not supposed to be an esoteric ramble that people could not possible understand, so let me just reiterating that you must, *absolutely MUST*, fill your mind with good information to maintain a healthy millionaire mindset.

People all too often, are quick to give away their assets also. This is not because they want to, it is because that they are not even aware that they are there within them.

A personal example. I know a few things about how the Internet works and about how to build a website, see even now I am playing things down.

I have just put together some content, an outline if you like, for an upcoming marketing event that I am speaking at, now I take what I know for granted, as do most people.

I racked my brain for a little bit to come up with what I was going to present, this was because I had too much information that would be useful... the thing is I don't know what people know, and what they are complete and utter numpties with (Technical term there).

My wife read what I had put together and she said, you're a knowledgeable son of a bitch aren't you?

I had trouble with this, as I thought that it was really simply logical and that most people would know it. And I can almost guarantee that you do the exact same thing! Everybody does, well 97% of the population it would seem.

I'm highlighting the fact that you literally have hidden *rivers of gold* running through your body. The truth is that there are things that you know inside and out, that other people know diddlysquat about, and of course this is true going both ways.

There is always someone somewhere that will be willing to pay you for the information that you have, the key is identifying what it is, and how to package it in a way where people will pay you for it.

The biggest issue you are going to face here is (and I have it too) is that you don't know what you know™, that or you simply don't know who you want to serve.

Yeah, I know, so lame, of course you *know what you know*... uh, NO, you don't, if you did have any idea what you knew or who you wanted to serve (who is your perfect client) you would have already used to make some pretty good money (OK maybe you know, but you don't know how to package it).

How then, do you find out what you know? Well a good way to start to get to the bottom of it is to create a list of things that you can do with your eyes shut (so to speak), things that come really easily to you, things that are like second nature.

Maybe you are great at organizing things around the home to make it more *'living friendly'*, maybe it is the fact that you can make bird calls with your hands... it really could be anything. Seriously start by making a list... go get a pen and paper.

Write down everything that comes into your head, no matter how absurd you think it is that you know it, or that you think everyone else knows it, just write it. You should be able to come up with a pretty good list.

These are things that you take for granted that you know. Once you have compiled a decent list, start looking through it and highlight at least three that you really enjoy, this is going to be important in the long run. The reason being is that when things get tough then you are going to want to quit, yet if it is something that you enjoy you are more likely to stick with it.

If you have done this I sincerely want to congratulate you as you are already in the top 10% of people who take action.

You already have a clearer picture of where I am going with this right now don't you? (Even if you don't that is ok) There is a point to all of this, you are going to have to trust me on this. What we have now done together is create the starting point for building up your empire (or whatever *you* want to call it).

Brendon Burchard takes a slightly different perspective when he talks about sharing your knowledge and expertise. He says that it could be something that you have a strong interest in, you might not necessarily have total mastery of it (seldom does anyone have total mastery of anything), yet you have a strong desire to learn more and become very proficient in whatever it is that you have an interest in. By learning more about your subject, it will not take long before you have considerable knowledge in that subject.

Take websites for an example, when I got started I didn't know HTML from PHP or FTP from java, yet I had a *ferocious curiosity* to learn how it all worked.

Are there still things that I don't know about the above? Absolutely there are, it just means there is more for me to learn which is fine. The point I make here is that I am now wise enough on the topic to be able to offer advice and strategies on web stuff to others who know less than me - and get paid for it.

I would not have been able to do any of this before had I not jumped in and learned more about something that fascinated me, and what do you know, I now speak on the topic.

Something very important to remember here is that the very thing that you make your own, may not have been done yet.

Cast your mind back to 2009/2010, or if you want to go back to very beginning 2004. 2004 is when *The Facebook* came to be, of course we now know this as Facebook.

Back to the first figures 2009/2010, then there was no such job position as *'Social Media Manager'* or *'Social Media Consultant'*, yet today (2014) it is one of the highest sought positions to be filled, and the reason for this is simple, there are not that many of them out there, well none that truly know how to do the job anyway, now this is changing, more and more people are learning the trade (so to speak) and getting their hands dirty and getting into *Social Media management*.

Do not get me wrong, I am not advocating a job, that being said, if it is simply a stay at home thing that you want to be able to do and get paid quite well for it, then this could be the ticket.

What I would advocate is learning how it is done, creating some systems around that and then training someone to do it for you, do this with two or more people and you have a team, then you can lease the team out and take a cut of what they earn, you get them the work with your reputation and take a commission of sorts for putting your team in work.

This might be slightly advanced (not really), however it may well have sparked an idea in your mind, and if it has then BOOM, job done! (sort of)

Before we can run we must first crawl (or as my youngest son did, walk on his hands and feet). There is more than likely some skill that you have, that right now has no particular use, that very well maybe something that people need to know.

As I have said, I remember hearing from a very successful associate of mine Chris Howard, and then he may have heard from another tall guy with big teeth, *it is never a matter of resources, it is a matter of resourcefulness.*

Take note, I am going to share with you very soon a way in which you can start to tap in on hose hidden *rivers of gold* running through your mind and body.

So far we have been through a few exercises in this book (hey no one said it was going to be easy, just that it would be worth it) and they all have a point, however they are pointless if you have not done them.

If so you might as well put this book on the shelf (or close your iBooks or Kindle app) and go grab some beer and fries. Everything that we have done so far build on itself, and the book has been put together in a logical sequence.

By now you really should have a good understanding of where your hidden rivers of gold may in fact lie. So now then we would want to begin to look at how we would go about creating a product from this and packaging it.

If your eyes are starting to roll in your head STOP it, stop it now! There is going to be a learning curve, however once that learning curve is learned, you are then going to look at getting someone else to do the *'hard yards'* for you, by this I mean you are going to hire, or contract, someone to build your products and even your websites.

I will be letting secrets out of the bag that could, potentially, put my Virtual Web Studio out of business.

That leaves you then to concentrate on quality control and increasing your knowledge (and creating new income streams as well).

Let's jump to the next chapter and start getting a look at what it is that we can create.

PACKAGING YOUR KNOWLEDGE

"A gentleman is one who puts more into the world than he takes out"
~*George Bernard Shaw*

In the *last* chapter we identified some possible (remember I said highlight at least three?) areas where your *Rivers of Gold* may be hiding. We want to take them that step further and create something tangible that you are able to sell and make money from.

Before we get head long into this, I want to point something out, what we are going to create here could very well be worth an extra $2,000-$5,000 a month, maybe not right away, however certainly over time. Once it is set up and operating, it is *almost* set and forget.

You may well be salivating at the mere thought of this, yet let me offer something more, for those of you who are a looking to *really crush this* and retire (remember my definition of retirement), it would be wise to look at this as an entry level product (anywhere from $27 per unit up to $197 per unit) that you are able to make a little money off of, perhaps by having affiliates promote it for you (More can be found about that in the resources section).

This is also as a way of beginning to build a database and start to build a relationship with these people. If they have brought this product that *you* have created, then chances are they would be interested in similar products or even products with a much higher value.

Not everyone will be interested in taking it to the next step (as in creating higher value products, but then, other people could do that for you), however it is important to know that this really is only an entry point to your marketing funnel, and this can lead to new income streams from it, so again, important to note.

I mentioned a database in the paragraph above, this is important. Here is why, if you have been around the Internet looking for ways to make money for any length of time then you would have heard the mantra; *'the money is in the list'*. And this is true, however despite what some people say, it does not necessarily have to be a HUGE list, in fact I know of people that have small lists and make a very comfortable living from them, due to the fact that these people have developed a relationship with their lists and in turn the list is very *responsive.*

If you can't be bothered building a relationship (not advised) then you are going to want a BIG list. If you are still in the dark about what a list is, simply put, it is a whole heap of people, who have *opted* into receive information from you, that you are able to send mail, email or gifts to over and over again that you can in turn generate an income from.

It is far more economical to market to people that have purchased from you before than it is to generate new customers, so that is something to consider.

I am breaking the following up in to a number of different parts. Consider the later parts to be that of bonus material where, if you were unable to think of something that you knew something about, however you have something that interests you and you know it to be a popular topic, then you still have a way in which you could pursue that and make an income from it also.

Option One

So our three potential *Rivers of Gold*? We are going to work on one at a time, in fact *we* are going to work on one and *you* are going to rinse and repeat.

So choose the one that *most resonates* with you, I know they all do, but the one that you would do above all else, and that it the one we are going to start with. The quickest and easiest (and usually the most economical) product to create is in fact an audio product.

And as with anything there are a number of ways in which you can do this. If you don't already have one then you are going to want to get yourself a headset with a microphone.

Because of my musical back ground I do have a pretty good vocal mic, however it really is not needed to produce a good quality recording, in fact more often than not I use a *Microsoft LifeChat*™ headset that has a built in microphone and it produces great sound.

This will more than likely set you back about $50 bucks or there a-bouts. If you want to try some out, then by all means find somewhere that will let you test it for your purposes and take it back to exchange it should it not perform the way you would expect it to, this is exactly what I did.

If you have seen any video of mine online, screen cast ones (i.e. not the ones where I am in front of the camera) then you will have heard me use the exact mic I describe above, and it works just fine.

You are also going to need something to be able to capture your voice to be able to create an audio. There are so many professional recording applications out there. They can range from a few hundred dollars right through to thousands of dollars.

I am mindful that you may be on a budget, so I am going to let you in on one of the worst kept secrets in Internet Marketing history, and that is *'Audacity'*, which you can find by heading over to http://audacity.sourceforge.net/ it is available for both Mac and PC users, and is a free open source piece of software that will allow you to record your voice.

This will be your basic studio set up, it is going to be most of what you need to be able to produce a product that you are able to then sell.

Once you have finished recording, you will be given a choice to export the file as a number of different file types; the one that we are really looking for is an .mp3 file. There may be times when you will need to output the file as a .WAV however for now an .mp3 will suffice.

What exactly will you be recording to make this wonderful audio program that you are going to be selling and solving people problems with? This will come down to the questions that need to be answered about your topic.

You may have a huge knowledge on a subject, this can be a two-edge sword as when you know so much about a particular topic, you can often take for granted what you know.

Perhaps there are questions that you want the answers to, this could be a great place to start, you could also hang out on Facebook, join groups that are associated with your topic and ask them what their top 3 questions about that subject are, before long you are going to have quite a bit of content to work from.

In fact you may very well have answered questions like this yourself, the chances are if you have, then you were helping someone with their marketing research. Congratulations!

Let's break that one down to see what I mean. So you are a mechanic by trade, you are working 60 hours a week, you love your work, but you hate the hours, you love cars and everything to do with them.

It would be safe to say that you have some knowledge about that subject. Who would be someone that would benefit from your knowledge? Most people right. There are a lot of people out there that do not have the first clue about push rods, con rods or pistons and valve stems.

You may have a particular fondness for porting engines to increase performance. Of course there are also others out there that would love to be able to do that yet do not know where to start. So you could very well create a *'step by step'* audio (or video, but that is getting ahead of ourselves) that walks someone through porting a polishing a cylinder head.

There is another market that we have not mentioned here at that would be ladies (not be chauvinistic, that is not the goal here), there are plenty of independent ladies out there that like to get their hands dirty, or even just want to know enough so they don't get screwed over by a mechanic that could be out to take advantage of them.

In that case you could create a simple audio (and check list) that they are able to work through to make sure they are getting the best deal and service that they can.

I heard of a gentleman that created a 'how to DVD' on *how to change a tire*, very simple to most people, yet a big enough market that, last I heard, was still making him $2,000 a month on auto pilot.

With everything you have available at your disposal today, then creating audio or even video can be a cinch. That is just one example, I am sure with that you can now even look at what you are currently doing for a job right now and think 'hold on, I could do….' And if that is the case that is great, even more creative juices flowing.

With audio you can also opt to carry out interviews with experts in the field or topic that you have chosen. There are literally thousands of people that would be willing to provide you with an interview for your product, why? Because, as with any interview, this will give them exposure and adds to their credibility, and you as the interviewee will provide them with a plug for their product or service. In fact there is a website dedicated to finding experts in your topic it is www.expertclick.com and you can quite honestly just search your *key word* and more than likely find hundreds of experts on your topic. If an interview is what you are going to do for your audio product then you are going to need another way to be able to record the interview, the beauty of the technology that we have these days is that you can interview someone on the other side of the world with ease. A great way in which you do this is through Skype, you will need to get yourself a third party add-on for Skype that will allow you to record your interview, so Audacity is not so good for this one, or if you were to do it through one of the countless free conference lines that you can get online, you would be able to record the call and download the file. The only problem that I have found with this is the quality of the recording is never that high, that is why I prefer Skype, as the call quality is usually pretty good. The recorders you can get for Skype *can* cost you money, however it is usually a one off investment, and certainly well worth it if you intend to conduct many interviews. The one I use with Skype is *'ecamm'* and it's for Mac, sorry this app is not available for PC. There is more software readily available for PC users at any rate, simply 'Google' Skype call recorders and see what you come up with, to let you know though, *ecamm* is a whopping investment of $29.95, it is hardly going to break the bank.

If you are going to simply do an audio (as opposed to an interview), then you might look at producing a six part (or CD) audio set, with each audio being about 40-60 minutes in length. Each one could be answering a particular question. Or if we use the examples as above it may be a different aspect of that task. Using our example of porting and polishing a cylinder head, it could be broken down by talking about all the ways in which you can surface the head. What tools you are going to need, what preparation work must be done in order to create the best results, lapping valve seats vs not lapping them etc.

You would be surprised that once you start talking on a subject that you are passionate about, and know a thing or two about how quickly the time can go by, and it really can be a matter of simply talking into the microphone without much preparation at all. This, in fact, produces something very authentic. That is not to say that you cannot re-record if you wanted to.

Great, so now you have completed your recording, and you have a raw product, what next? Well you are going to want to get some graphics done for it and you are also going to want a place where you are able to have the orders fulfilled from. I am going to cover this a little more as I wrap this chapter up due to the fact that with some of the other things you can do to get a start with this income stream will also tie in with where you get the graphics done, where to get your products prettied up for sale and where you can get your audios transposed so that you can also add a manual, or written transcripts to your product increasing its perceived monetary value.

What mentioned here is the fact that doing an interview or creating a short 40 minute audio on *'the top 7 things everyone should know about your topic before purchasing anything else'* is also a great way of creating a *lead magnet* to be able to start building your (*opt in*) list to be able to market to over and over again. One of the bonuses you are entitled to with the investment in this book is my video course *'The List Crusher'* which shows you how you can build a list quickly. This normally retails for *$47*, however it is yours free at www.RiversOfGold.com.au/bonuses it will be a great way for you to be able to learn how you can build your list and maintain it in such a way that your customers will be rabid waiting to hear what you have to offer them next. (OK, maybe not *rabid*, excited though)

Option Two

The second easiest thing to create that I would suggest would be an eBook with the information that you have, or that you are going to research.

You don't know the first thing about making an eBook? It is ok; we are going to run through it.

Keep in mind why someone would want your eBook to begin with... and that is simple. Just the same as a traditional business, you are solving a problem or providing information on a certain way of doing things that someone has an interest in, yet does not necessarily know how it all works.

Very similar to our audio product that we just spoke about before. There is a chance that you have purchased one yourself, if so, why? It was more than likely to answer a question that you had, or that you wanted to learn something new.

This is a great starting point as now that you know your eBook is going to be written to answer questions, you can then start to compile a list of common questions that need answers (or do what was suggested before, join associated Facebook groups, or other forums, and ask questions). There are a couple of things you can do here, you can research and find the answers to these questions (you may even know the answers to them), or you can outsource this and have someone else research and answer the questions and then format it into an eBook and provide you with the files. If you choose to research the topic yourself you may also want to type the content out, which is fine, although if you have not made one before then it may be easier (and less time consuming) to have someone do it for you. You can find such people at www.oDesk.com or www.elance.com.

If you were to use the services here then you would simply post a job listing stating what you were looking for, i.e. someone to either research and create and eBook or someone to simply format the content that you have into an eBook. If you are hell bent on doing it all yourself (and I can be stubborn like that too) then there are *pages and pages of information online* that can help you, and this information is there freely, you just may have to hunt a little for it.

I say that is due to the fact that there are courses that you can buy, and while I am all for buying courses, save your investment for a bigger and better course, writing an eBook is not too hard, and there is plenty of free information out there that can help you do exactly that!

Let us assume that you have asked what people's top questions are about your subject, and let's say that you are unsure, or don't have the time to be able to sit down and answer all of these questions. Then as stated previously you can have someone do it for you.

You can provide them with what you think are the top ten questions that you received and asked them (pay them) to go out and research this, they then put the information into an eBook format and create all the files that you need in order to be able to give your eBook away or start selling it, this does not include your website, and we can get to that soon, just know that you can have someone do the bulk of this work for you.

This could be anywhere from $50 to $1,000 dependent on who you get to perform the job. We will go into more depth on that a little later.

Option Three

Again, with advances in technology and the things that we have at our disposal like mobile phones, Skype, eBook readers etc... there really is so much scope, and there is scope to be able to recycle a lot of what you create and get more mileage from it all.

A good friend of mine, a business coach, said it to me like this once,

"You want to try and create products, or reports, that have a lot of legs"

Basically saying that if you create something, certainly in the digital, or information world, you should create it in such a way where you are able to recreate it in different formats, like our audio, you can also have it transcribed and then you have a report… you could, conceivably, then turn that report into a power point presentation and create a video for it (I will more than likely turn this book into an audio book, and it is available as both a printed book and an eBook). See what I mean? This is not necessarily something that you would do with all of your products, however you could do it with content that you were making as a free offer as a way to build your lists.

I have mentioned technology, well most mobile phones these days, certainly smart phones, have the capability of recording very high quality video, some even allow for the editing of that video right there on your phone! So then how easy is it now to be able to capture teaching moments when you are out and about?

You might know countless facts about finding the perfect property to move in to, what to look for to make sure that you are not buying a lemon, how to negotiate with the vendor or agent, you may very well be looking at a house and have a great teaching moment come up, you bring out your phone and you capture it. You are now on your way to creating a product.

Don't worry if you don't know how to edit it to make it all look pretty, or even how to format it to make it into a DVD file (complete with menu etc…) to send to your product fulfillment house, visit one of the sites already mentioned and you will be able to find someone who will do it for you for pennies on the dollar.

Using a camera is only *one* way that you could create a DVD or video course, maybe you know how to create a really schmick presentation in keynote (Mac) or power point (PC), so you deliver your content that way, make a presentation, use the mic that you got for your audio and then get a screen capture software, the industry standard is *Camtasia*, however there are a number of different ones out there, and you can even find open source ones that cost you nothing to download and use.

So you shoot your video, and again, if you want someone to format it for you, find them on one of the sites (or search for outsource contractors) and provide them with the brief for what you want and the raw files to put together.

Asking someone, or rather contracting someone to do this for you is not lazy, it is perfectly legitimate, and further more, if you are serious about creating more income streams it will become more and more important to manage your business and your time.

It frees you up to concentrate on expanding what you are doing and thinking up new cool products for people to invest in.

So there are three different ways that you can take to the bank right now, of making a product. Believe me, people are doing this every day, you may very well have heard stories of people making millions of dollars a week, even a day, well *it is possible*, and people *are doing it*.

There is a very well-known Internet marketer who created an info product that effectively taught sales with the use of NLP, the product was available for the princely sum of $1,997. This product (of which I have a copy and LOVE it) grossed *over $28,000,000 in the first 48 hours* of it being on sale. So yeah, you can make good money online and quickly.

I am not telling you this so that you get all starry eyed and go *"Yeah I am going to make a million dollars"* the truth is you could, yet the reality is that you won't.

You, if you take action, could very well create a passive income stream that will be worth a lot more over time, this is something that will help you take vacations every year and put the kids through school, it could even get you that new car every year. It really is up to you. No the reason I am telling you this is because there will be plenty of people out there that will tell you that your crazy, what are you doing that for… you know you have heard it.

These are the people that are scared you are going to leave them behind, they are scared that *you* will change, it's not that you will change, it is that you will *grow*. These people, these *well-meaning* people, will ultimately destroy your dreams… *if* you let them.

With the exercises and such that you have done in this book, you will be building up a fair inventory of information that you can use to help yourself create and generate multiple streams of income, and you should by now be getting some great ideas on ways to improve on what has been shown here also. That is the thing with anything that you do, no matter how much knowledge or know how about a subject that you have, as soon as you start talking to someone else, or reading as you are now, about information you always get little ideas and *'aha'* moments that pop into your head, take advantage of those, and write them down, an idea is fleeting, you may only ever have it once, that is why I had to get out of bed to start writing it, I was so excited!

As a little bit of an extra here, I want to add this; as you go about what you are doing, *document it*, journal about what you have done throughout your day. The systems you have put in place, the certain way in which you have done things, whether that is research or whatever, this is going to make it easier when it does come time to outsource your work, and believe you are going to want to eventually, no matter how much you enjoy it, you are simply not going to have the time to be able to do it all.

Getting Your Product

Earlier in this chapter I mentioned about what to do with your product when you had recorded it. You are obviously going to want to market it and get it selling.

I cover building a website etc. in the next chapter, however here I wanted to cover off about finding someone, or somewhere that will fulfill your order and actually package and create (put the audio, movie or document files, into their respective delivery mechanism) your product.

There are companies out there that will do all of this for you. I *could* sit here and give you a list, however you should know how to fish by now, so go and Google product fulfillment and 'interview' some prospective fulfillment partners.

If you wanted to, you can use the contractors that you have found to structure the raw files of your products into whatever format that you wanted to deliver it to your fulfillment house so that when an order comes in, they simply press, print and deliver.

Brendon Burchard gives a great example of how to do this in his audio for the *'Experts Academy'*, do yourself a favor and check it out.

GETTING ONLINE

"The Internet is becoming the Town Square for the global village of tomorrow".
~Bill Gates.

You will have more than likely noticed a pretty common theme throughout this book. That is one of an *online type scenario*.

The reason for this, in case it is not obvious, is merely for the fact that this is where a majority the worlds millionaires, and in fact, billionaires are going to come from over the next few years, and many of them from humble beginnings, remember Google? They started in a garage, as did Apple computers, now look at them, Apple is the world's second largest company, it, at last check, had over $178,000,000,000 in cash. In case you can't figure out the zeros on there, that is 178 Billion dollars.

It is also the most economical way to get your start, we will look at other ways to develop income streams in other books throughout the series, and this is really to help you start, and making some money.

When I refer to online I am not just talking about desktop computers, I am talking about *mobile devices*, they are really in their infancy in the capabilities that they will have. And already they are very capably, in fact, this chapter (as with others in this book) are being written on a mobile device.

So when we are discussing online presence here in this chapter then you can take it that we are referring to mobile devices as well. There may be times in this chapter where I will refer directly to mobile and or a desktop computer.

Firstly I want to touch on the *web real estate* that is available, and it is definitely a good idea to be thinking of a website (whether it is owned by you or not) as real estate. If you were in the brick and mortar world, you would have hard costs; the beauty of being online is that those hard costs are a lot less.

When you look at your endeavors like this it does two things, it makes you thankful that you don't have a bricks and mortar business, and creates a mindset that can give you the edge before you begin.

If you were to do a spread sheet for your projections on costs profits and losses, then you would quickly see how inexpensive working online can be.

Let's say that you have a shop selling soap, it is boutique and you already have a good reputation, people come from all over the country to see your wears.

You have a shop in a great location so you pay the rent that matches. Let say that your rent is $4,000 a month (actually quite cheap, a small spot in a Westfield shopping centre will start from $2,500 a week), you have electricity and a phone that you have to also consider. We'll say that is $250 a month. Now we have a total of $4,250 a month.

In very, very, basic terms you have to make that each and every month before you even look like making a profit. Compare that to an online business, you have the same sort of cult following and you now can cater to the overseas market also. You obviously need a website, you will need a customer relationship system (CRM), a domain name and hosting. That covers the basics (just as we did in the shop example). Your domain is charged (or leased to you) at a yearly rate, let's call it $25 pa (Based on a .com extension far more expensive than normal), hosting, say $120 pa, so if we break those two down we can go on with the other things, so a domain $25 divided by 12 months = $2.08 per month, hosting, $120 divided by 12 months = $10 per month, customer relationship software $99 per month, and your website, well this can vary greatly, with most hosting plans you can add a Wordpress platform to your domain very easily, you can also get any number of free themes for your Wordpress site or purchase one from many premium them sites. Let's say you paid someone to do it for you, and let's say that it cost you $997 (as that is what my web studio do websites for) divide that now over 12 months also, $997 divided by 12 months = $83.08 (and once 12 months is up this cost disappears). Adding all of this together we get our monthly figure;

$194.16 a month as opposed to $4,250. A real saving of $4,055.84.

That is money that you can invest to expand your business. OK, so the latter of that example are real prices of what your hard costs are for operating a 'shop' online, if not slightly inflated. If you look at this in context it is not hard to see why so many bricks and mortar shops are going out of business. They simply can't compete with the prices online shops are able to offer.

A real life example of my own. I have an iPad 2, this is in fact what I am writing this on right now. I clearly have an external keyboard (can you imagine trying to type a book on the built in keyboard?). I purchased this from Big W, and I did it, as I wanted it NOW.

I looked at a couple of different options, I would have liked an aluminum hard cased keyboard, however at Big W they were in excess of $100 and knew that I would more than likely find one online cheaper. There is nothing wrong with the keyboard that I have now, I mean I am typing right? For all intents and purposes it is all the keyboard I need, yet I still wanted the aluminum one.

So I looked on line, and what do you know, I managed to get one, that was identical (I mean right down to the packaging) to the one I saw in Big W, for $39.95 (and some were even cheaper) with free shipping, a free stylus, head phones and an extra USB cord for an iPad.

You see there is a big difference, a saving of over 60%. The only reason that they are able to do this at this price is due to the fact they do not have the same overheads as a traditional business does. Over 50% of all purchases in 2011 in the US were made online. So, metaphorically speaking *"Get busy living, or get busy dying".*

What I really want to go through here in this chapter is getting yourself a website, and why it is important not to be reliant on external sites like Facebook, YouTube, eBay, basically any site that you are not in total control over.

The reason is as simple as it is obvious, and that is if there is something the aforementioned sites don't like, or worse someone complains about your page, store, channel or whatever, then they can (and will) shut you down in a heartbeat. I know of a successful young lady here on the Gold Coast who had in excess of 100,000 fans on Facebook as was shut down overnight due to a 'complaint'.

All of these sites are great for traffic generation to your websites, however should not be used in solitary. You absolutely must maintain a control of your web assets. That may mean that you hire a web master

, it may not, who knows. It depends on your aspirations and how far you want to grow this thing, and really the only limit there is to what you can do here is the limit that you place upon it, or yourself.

I am sure that if you started to look around the Internet you would find plenty of people telling you that setting up a basic landing page for a website is difficult.

Granted there are certain ways that you can do things that are harder than others, and these points can be important and should not be ignored, however initially we are looking at setting up on a budget right? So the basics will prevail here.

I am going to give a brief run down on a landing page and how you can quickly set one up, I am going to show you how you can get your hands a little dirty in code, and also where you can find a place where you can simply 'drag and drop' to build a page.

If all of this looks or sounds like it is going over your head, worry not as I will also be including the link to some videos in the resources section of this book for you to be able to follow along step by step and build your own.

Remember our product that we talked about previously? I remember learning very early on in my online business life, that for each and every product that you create you it should have its own domain name. What I mean by that is if your product was called 'Scrap Booking in a Minute' then your domain would be www.ScrapBookinginaMinute.com. Your product deserves its own page; it would look silly if you had another domain name with an extension on it, like this www.AnotherDomain.com/ScapBookingInAMinute/.

It, among other things makes you look like you are cheap; I mean really, you can get a .com domain for no more than $12 per annum (most of the time less).

Important to note here that when you are registering a domain that you really want to do it for at least 2 years, the reasoning behind this is one of legitimacy. Often if I am simply securing a domain name for future use, I will just register it for 12 months, however if I start using it then I extend the lease. Your site is more likely to be treated like a spam site (with no legitimacy) if it is registered for any less than 2 years at a time. This will hurt your chances of reaching the top of the search engines as they (well mainly Google, let's face it) believe that if you have only registered your domain for one year then you are not serious about what you are selling or if you're not selling anything, the information that you are providing will have no real value.

Your Own Website

Then where do we begin? Well I could say that you could start by opening note pad (or text edit in plain text format) and tell you that the first tag you need to type is *<html>* and then *<head>* Put your key words and such in here then close it like *</head>* and then *<body>*. The write whatever you want to write, and then when finished close the tags in reverse order like this *</body>* and then *</html>*. That is really basic html, however that is not what I am going to do,

You can also simply use a WP theme to be able to build a good landing page for you too. I mean there are ways to do this on the cheap, let me explain.

It is important to think about what function your website has, is it simply your store? Are you setting it up to sell one item or more?

Continuing with what we have already looked at *i.e. creating a product to sell* (rather than importing goods to sell in an online store, another income stream altogether). With that in mind then your site is basically going to consist of no more than 6 pages really.

Your landing (or squeeze) page, your offer page, and your download page. OK so three pages there, the others may come into play later, but for now that will get us started.

Your Landing Page, the Squeeze.

You could be forgiven for thinking to yourself, what they heck is a squeeze page. In essence it is the first page that someone comes to when they are visiting your offer. It is where you are going to start to *'qualify'* your prospects.

They have found your page by whatever means and now you want to give yourself the best chance of affecting the sale. The most common thing that someone would expect to see in a landing page these days is a video, people want the information, and they want to assimilate it easily.

You will have about 5-7 seconds in which to capture someone's attention, after that they have more than likely clicked off and are on someone else's page by now, you have to give them a reason to stay.

Something that is going to entice them to fill in their real details so that you are able to communicate with them.

You Absolutely MUST provide value here, otherwise you are just another *'also ran'*. There is every chance that you have even put your name and email in on a similar page to get information that you wanted to know.

You may have even done it in the lead up to getting this book. So the idea is to encourage people to leave their details (again, there is information on this in the list crusher) so that you are able to begin a dialogue with them.

As with most sales situations, there are at least six touch points that you want to think about, or should have before you can expect to make the sale.

You are saying to yourself...

"Dialogue? Andrew you said that this was a hands off type approach, you know passive income!"

And you would be right, I did say that, and I am definitely an advocate for it. If you cast your mind back though (or go back and read it, you know you highlighted it), I also said that there might be some work in the initial stages.

If you went through the system that ultimately 'sold' this book, then you have in fact been through something similar, and I am sorry if I am shattering an illusion here, however all of the work for that system was done well before the book was published, yet it is still working today (assuming I have not stopped selling the book).

So setting up your landing page also includes setting up all of your auto responders and offers etc... that you may like to include over a 12 months period, again writing all of the content for this can be outsourced, however I would encourage you to at least write the first six (six touch points), they don't have to be long, however they should have at least three links inside (top, middle and end) that link back to your offer (sales) page.

This is to give them an opportunity to purchase if they have not, so the copy should be written that would entice them to do so.

The Offer (Sales Page)

Your prospects have made it past your landing page, they have confirmed their information, and now they are looking at your sales page.

This is where you have to give them all the reasons why they would want to invest in your product... in effect you answer their questions by imagining what they would be and simply writing them.

Copy writing is a skill, some people have it naturally, and some have to work for it. Again included in the members area of the site mentioned in the *Resource Section* of this book is a whole course on copy writing, and as a member it is free for you to access.

Obviously the idea of a sales page is to get the sale, and the ones that you miss should be picked up with your email sequence (auto responders) that comes out after people have visited your site. There would be enough information there for someone to be able to make an informed decision about your particular product, however not so much that they get all the information they need not to have to purchase your products... now this is more about sales psychology, and that is most certainly NOT what this book is about. Remember the copywriting course included in the member's area.

Your offer (sales) page has a certain structure to it that will ensure that you maximize your chances of making a sale on the first visit. Australia's (self-professed) highest paid copywriter, he makes about $750,000 a year on autopilot has a formula that he calls B.U.R.P.I.E.S. which breaks down like this;

Big Promise (the headline needs to grab attention)

Use Imagination (use the consumer's own imagination… 'Imagine being able to…')

Rarity (everyone values something that is rare or a limited number of)

Points (this is where you would list out the benefits of your product)

Irresistible Offer (but wait there is more… buy now and you get a set of Ginsu steak knives!)

Evidence (customer testimonials, REAL ones, you can trade copies of your products to get testimonials etc…)

Sign Off (this is where you would put your call to action and price, again in the copywriting course)

Or you can use the old A.D.I.A. formula

Attention, grab peoples attention with a bold statement

Desire, engage peoples desire about a certain (your certain) product

Imagination, engage peoples imagination, have them see themselves in the possession of your product or service.

Action, give a clear call to action as to what you would like your new customer to do next.

That is basically your offer or sales page, pretty simple right? Don't be overwhelmed, once again you can outsource this if you want to or can afford to… the investment to get this done can vary… some copywriters know their worth and charge appropriately.

Thank You Page

Once your prospect has made their order you are going to want them to be able to get instant access to the product you have created. So after 'checkout' you will want them redirected to the thank you (or download) page, this is where you can remind them that they are now on your list, you can thank them for their custom, you can let them know what to expect to see on their credit card statements (this will reduce charge backs).

A note on that, do not be afraid to back what you say up with a money back guarantee, unless you have one these days you will only sell a small amount anyway, however this gives piece of mind, and the amount of returns you get are minimal so long as you are providing good content that helps the customers who purchased.

If you are also doing your email sequencing right you will be building trust and rapport at any rate, which, just like traditional business, will reduce returns and unhappy customers also.

You will also want to protect your downloads as much as you can, if your link is not encrypted and your product turns out to be a hot seller, it will not take long for someone to leak out your download link and then your hard work will be gone! For Free…

If you decide to use a Wordpress platform there are plugin ins that will protect your downloads for you etc… otherwise you will need to get a script that will do it for you and more than likely have to pay someone to set it up for you… unless you are prepared to get your hands dirty in code and learn a complex programming language. No?

Web Property

Now you have built your site, then what? With the social media presence that is available today, keeping in mind what I said near the start of the chapter, you would be mad not to capitalise on it.

So absolutely use the social networks to get the word out, build a page on Facebook, open a YouTube channel, create a twitter feed, these are all great places that you are able to generate traffic to your site. This is not a book on how to do social media, this is merely one that would spur you into taking action, there are heaps of resources online where you can learn social media strategies, look up a gentle man by the name of *Michel Q Todd*, he is the man when it comes to twitter, and I know he has some other great tips that would certainly help you with your online effort.

So there are also other sites that are not so well known, well certainly to people that are not into Internet marketing... yet. Places like *Squidoo*, which is a place where you can create what they call a 'lens', you pretty much create a web page within their ecosystem, which has great creditability with Google, to 'pre-sell' your product and then link it to your page, this can be done with pretty much anything, even (and quite often especially) affiliate offers.

Although this is not meant to be a 'Internet marketing' book, there are a couple of things also that you will want to do, one of which is simple and easy... and that is write articles, again training available in the members area, basically you want content out there that is going to point back to your site providing you with a 'backlink'.

I really want to give you the information so you can get to get yourself out there making money... however I can't do it justice here, as this really is a book, or course even, in itself. I know some of the information just shared here is possibly a little dry, I know this as it was hard to motivate to write it, as it is stuff that I know and take for granted. Yet I know the significance of some of what I have shared may have been missed by some, if that is you, then do not let it discourage you. You don't necessarily need to know all of that information, it is more a nice to know, who knows, you might have caught a bug that makes you want to learn more about coding etc...

GET READY? BE READY!

"Opportunities multiply as they are seized."
~Sun Tzu

People talk all the time about getting ready for the 'big thing' that is coming, whatever that 'big thing' is. That is part of the problem;

1. They are *talking* about it, and;

They are getting ready.

This goes back a little bit to our mindset, yet it is pertinent to share this, particularly towards the end of this book, as it is one of the most important, if not *the* most important aspects of anyone's success.

All too often people miss the most basic and simple of opportunities that have the power to change their life in unimaginable ways, all because they are 'getting ready' for that big break or that big opportunity, or whatever event they think is coming.

The secret is not to be 'getting ready' it is simply to *be ready*. This does come back to the *Be Do Have* principle that we touched on, and even though I said I would go against convention and not include it, I have included here in this chapter the article I said to search for, here in its entirety and original format;

It is safe to say that one of the very the corner stones of Personal Development is the principle of BE, DO and HAVE.
You hear it all the time, be the person you want to be, do the things that person does and then you will have their results. I have spoken of this before and it something that has been bugging me, why has it been bugging me? It was bugging me for one simple reason, when I first heard it, I was open to it, and in fact it made perfect sense. As I began to put into practice the principles of BE DO HAVE I immediately got results. Wow I thought, how simple is this, why are not more people using this simple philosophy? Obviously it works! There are any number of reasons why people are not using the principle, fear, lack of faith, self-doubt. These

would be the most common. I want to go back to my experience however, and the reason for this is quite simply because I was not actually using the principle correctly, and because of this I inadvertently caused a few people a bit of frustration, and for this I do sincerely apologise. Those people should know who they are, and if not, my thoughts are with them regardless. As I have previously posted, I have not always got it right, and I really do need to be, and am truly thankful for that, as if that had not happened I would have never really seen how the BE DO HAVE principle really works.

I spoke with a friend of mine today by the name of Kurek Ashley, this is a guy who really knows what it's like to have been down and climbed back up, he is a shining example of what 'can be'. For those of you who have not heard of Kurek he is a 'Peak Performance' coach, he coached the (mindset of the) Australian Woman's Olympic Beach Volley Ball team to a gold medal at the 2000 Sydney Olympics. He gives one of the best examples of the BE DO HAVE principle on his book 'How Would Love Respond?' in Chapter 11 'The Fortune Teller'. I suggest if you have not read this book that you must!

If anyone knows about pain and suffering Kurek does, and as he said to me today,

"I've been down the road of being at the bottom, there is nothing new for me to experience there".

If you were not looking for it, or did not quite understand the BE DO HAVE principle then you might well miss the message, not that it is not written well, in fact the contrary can be said, no what I mean, is that if you are not ready for the message, you may not see it right away.

I listened to the wake up to success call this morning with Tony Rush from Liberty League international, and he had a guest on the call, another person that I am blessed enough to call my friend, Shannon Lavenia. Now what Shannon and Tony were talking about was about playing games and being able to create cash on demand because of the games. It was very entertaining and very insightful. She also highlighted the very heart of the BE DO HAVE principle. It was because of this that I finally could see the easiest way of explaining it.

When you are in a state of BEing, a lot of us miss the point. Some of us think that acting in the certain way is BEing, and I guess in part that is true. For me however I think the best way of BEing is by living in the end result let me say that again just to sink in;

Living in the end result

For Natalie Cook, 2000 Olympic Gold Medallist, it was buying her display cabinet for her gold medal 3 years prior to winning it.

It is BEing able to live in that moment, even though that moment may be years away. It is BEing able to stay true to your outcome in spite of what others are saying or doing to cause adversity.

To me, and of course this is my opinion, to be able to see your future so clearly and vividly in spite of what is actually happening around you, and actually living with a *knowingness that what you are doing is the right thing and that it will produce amazing results is where your power lies.*

When you are consistent with BEing then the DOing becomes a part of your natural flow, and therefore you must HAVE the Results.

Never ever let go of that clarity and vision, for the moment you do, you have a long climb to get back to where you were. It will not be insurmountable, however it may take more time.

I cannot explain it any simpler than that.

I want to leave you with something Buddha said;

'There is no way to happiness. Happiness is the way'
~ Buddha

That was my take on the Be, Do, Have.

The context of what I am saying here is that living in your end result mentally will cause things to show up in your physical world a lot more rapidly, therefore *being ready* rather than 'getting ready' is important.

I mentioned that when you are in a state of 'getting ready' that you may well miss simple and easy opportunities to make money, or dramatically change your life for the better. When you are in a state of *being ready* then opportunities just appear, keep in mind they may very well have been there before, however as you were 'getting ready' you missed them.

In effect when you are in a state of 'getting ready' you are actually '*getting ready to get ready*'. It means that you are in state of readiness however you more than likely don't know what you are getting ready for, and then this subconscious thought becomes the proverbial dog with a bone, it won't let it go and subsequently clouds the vision and causes you, as stated above, to miss what you may well need to succeed.

So then what does *being ready* look like as opposed to 'getting ready'? Many of the successful people I know have all had times where they flux between the two.

An example could be this; when I was starting *The Affordable Website Co* I set up the whole site, I set the price list, I set up the entire shopping cart, I made the thing work, and I did the work. This of course was unsustainable if I was to grow the business and work on other things that were important to me (like writing this book).

I kept thinking that there was something else that I needed to learn before I would be able to step back to a more project management type role... I was *getting ready*. As I was tied up and investing all my time in learning things, that for all intents and purposes, I knew, I was unable to see new opportunities that came and went, or at least I did not have the capacity to see a way of doing them as all my time was taken up on getting the site up and doing the dog work.

Once I got into a state of *being ready* then I was able to look at the project objectively, I could see that by managing the project builds and directing traffic, so to speak, I was not only able to see more possibilities within the business itself and more opportunities too, I was also able to provide a better service at a better price, which is great for my customers and even better for the company growth and expansion.

So what life changing things could you be missing simply from being in a state of 'getting ready'? You could miss opportunities like speaking in front of a thousand people that are in the market for the information that you have to offer, you could miss talking to the very person that knows the someone that you desperately want to talk to and interview, you could miss talking to the very person that has the ability to invest in your proposition to reach into a market that you have been looking at. In essence it is in the 'listening' of the people that you talk to. When you are 'getting ready' people may tell you things that could help you and you miss them, or dis-miss them, because you are 'not ready yet'.

Another example of being ready that I have recently had was while I was having a meeting with an online acquaintance with whom I had spoken to regularly online, we lived in the same region, yet we had never caught up for a coffee or a lunch or anything… more than likely as I was in a state of 'getting ready' rather than being ready. We caught up as we had plenty of friends in common and thought it was about time that we did just that. During our lunch there was conversation about certain business opportunities that we had both seen over time and some of the people that were involved and how they postured themselves one way yet *acted* another.

" What you do speaks so loudly that I cannot hear what you say" ~Ralph Waldo Emerson

---

It was around this time that my friend said something that piqued my interest even further. And that was about a new car (an $80,000 BMW) that he was driving that he in effect paid $1,300 dollars for... I say in effect as he paid for the car with money he had generated from an original investment of $1,300 over a seven-month period.

Now having played in the investment sector in a previous life (and from seeing what is out there *if* you look), I understood the rule of compounding interest, and then he told me he was getting a 2% daily return on investment (ROI). That is for every $10 advertising position that you could purchase, you would be paid .20c. Pretty simple math, yet when you add a compounding factor into that it does not take long to generate a decent sort of return and when done in the right way, becomes a self-sustaining beast... kind of the like the holy grail of passive income. Just for an example if you purchased ten $10 positions ($100) and did nothing with it for 12 months you would have a potential return of $17,400 or a daily return of $340 dollars, ok so $340 dollars a day does not sound like that much, however when you consider that you only purchased ten $10 positions (remember $100?) it is pretty fantastic. In fact most people would tell you that it is 'too good to be true', remember that little chestnut? (We spoke of it in the first or second chapter) Yet this is actually happening, I have experienced it myself and seen it it with my own eyes. These sorts of returns are available (wealthy people have known this for years) each and every day, they are not illegal, they are not Ponzi schemes or pyramids, no simply legitimate ways in which you can create real financial independence.

Had I been in state of 'getting ready' I might well have missed that, the fact that I was in a state of *being ready* created a whole world of new opportunities that were not possible before learning of that opportunity.

There is something within what I have written above that I really need to address. There are unscrupulous individuals and even companies that will take advantage of you, and yes there *are* illegal activities out there that will also claim to give you a high return, and you will end up on the losing end.

Make sure that you exercise due diligence, if there is one thing that I have learned through my business life, it is that.

And the end of the day you are responsible for your actions, if more people realised that and lived by that then this world might be an easier place to live.

How can you make sure you are in a state of *being ready* as opposed to 'getting ready'?

If you have a knowingness about your end result, you have set your goals, you understand them, you have your big picture and are open to the things that are going on around you and the *listening* thereof, then it is probably safe to say that you are in a state of *being ready*.

That is not to say that you can then sit back and cruise, no, this is something that you will want to continually check in with, I know that I have to, it is very easy to become complacent and put you back into a state of 'getting ready'. Having doubt in *what you know* will put you back there faster than you can blink, that is why I talk about the fact that *'you don't know what you know'*™.

If you want to clear that up for yourself ask four of the people you trust the most, and who know you well, and ask them to tell you what it is that they think you know, you will begin to get an idea.

So go out, *BE* ready and things will just happen, can't explain it, like why the posi-track on the rear end of a Plymouth works or the sun sets, it just does.

4.5 TRILLION REASONS WHY

There are many reasons you might want to consider creating multiple income streams, and through out this book we have explored some of those whys and even a few of the hows. Practically all of them require input or management on your part. What if there was a way that you could shorten the learning curve on something and benefit quicker, with little to NO input after the fact?

What I am about to share with you is one of the most guarded income streams that there is available to you. There are many, many people that would not want you to have even a snippet of the information I am about to share with you. And they truly are $4,500,000,000,000 very good reasons that this would be something that you would want to consider when investigating where you would like to park, or invest money with the possibility of some very good returns.

On any given day in the Foreign Exchange (FX) market, there is approximately $4,500,000,000,000 traded (or there a-bouts, its between 4-5 trillion). Which means it is about 10,000 times bigger than practically all the other markets (stocks, commodities, options, etc...) combined. The flow on from that is that it makes it one of the hardest markets to manipulate.

It is a highly leveraged market, which basically means that you can do a lot with a little. Meaning you can make a heck of a lot of money with a small amount... sadly the opposite of that is also true, you can lose a lot of money with a little.

The statistics are not that pretty. 96% of all FX traders fail, and fail miserably. And of the 4-5% of traders that actually win from the market 50% of their trades lose. The good thing about that is the fact that the good traders, the really *great* traders can even make a losing trade a winning trade.

I have a mentor that has made his fortune in trading the markets, his father taught him options trading when he was seven. By the time he was 22 years old he had 'retired' from his accounting profession as a millionaire. He made the bulk of his fortune in trading FX. Of course he has prudently diversified his investment portfolio and has multiple income streams. I asked him if he would teach me the ins and outs of trading... his response was;

"Yeah for sure, so long as you are going to commit ten years to perfecting it?"

He was dead serious. He explained to me that all of the good traders that he knew all had a minimum of ten years trading experience. He said that there were people out there that might have a good trading record for the short term, he explained to me that it was pretty easy to fudge the numbers for the short term. He told me that he would not look at a trader who had less than ten years experience. For the simple fact that he has seen enough traders to know what is going to make the trader money, and what is not.

There are also brokers out there that full well know the statistics on traders, i.e. 96% of them fail, they run 'dealer desks' and basically wait for the trades to come in and place trades the opposite of what you placed. Is this legal? Yes unfortunately it is, it is ethical or fair? No, not really.

This is *partially* why people are so fearful about FX and the markets as a whole. And also one of the reasons that people have such a hang up about trusting people who make a lot of money. We have spoken about this repeatedly throughout this book, society has indoctrinated the majority to *think* a certain way. It really is not in their best interests to have you being able to think for yourself.

After reading all of that, you could be forgiven for thinking;

'what the hell? Why would I want to play in *that* market then, its full of vipers and thieves'

Its not all doom and gloom. Remember the 4-5% or traders that win about 50% of the time? Their 50% wins equal huge amounts of potential revenues.

I am not a financial planner, and I do not know your own particular circumstances. FX may very well be something that you should well avoid. Then again it may very well be one piece of the financial jigsaw puzzle you are trying to put together. I have personally seen returns of between 2-9% a month compounding. Make no mistake this *is* an investment and I am NOT providing you with personal investment advice, merely highlighting the fact that this is out there and people are making millions from it each and every year. Einstein summed compound interest up like this;

"Compound interest is the eighth wonder of the world. He who understands it, earns it ... he who doesn't ... pays it."
~Albert Einstein

The fact remains that if you are not somehow involved, or educating yourself on FX then you are missing a big portion to the multiple income stream pie.

Back to my mentor, he told me I needed ten years experience to be proficient at it... so why would I say that you should educate yourself? Simple, it is always good to have at least a working knowledge of what you are going to look at. And it may be something that you really enjoy and get into, you could very well be the 4-5% of people that turn into an amazing trader.

You may now also be thinking;

'Wait a minute Andrew, you said that this was truly passive, that it could be run with little to no input from myself'

To which I would say you are 100% correct and thank you for remaining alert and attentive. I said to my mentor that I really wanted a working understanding of it, and I did not want to be sitting in front of a screen trading FX every day 5.5 days a week, particularly when there was a high chance my trades would fail anyway, was there a way I could still benefit from FX?

I mean there are countless 'guru's' out on the circuit that are selling their trading courses telling all the punters how easy it is... when the truth is only about 4% of them make any money at all, which could also then be argued that they are the same 4% of the populous that would likely work it out on their own at any rate. Was there a way?

He told me there was and that by doing it this way, it would practically make it a passive investment, so again I am not giving out investment advice, I am simply highlighting that there are systems available where you can effectively have a professional trade your account for you.

Using the same systems that has and continues to provide them with a great income where they do what they do full time because they love it... however they have set themselves up in such a way that it removes all the emotions from the trading.

This is key to winning or losing, they have their trading rules that they have developed overtime which means that they can practically predict what results they are going to have. Most countries regulate this market and make it very clear that they are not legally able to offer or even suggest what *will* happen with the market, they cannot *speculate* as to how your account will perform, and neither they should, this is something that you, and only you, can decide on getting involved in.

What they can do is provide you with past performance, again this is *not* indicative of future performance, however it might give you some insight into how things *might* go for you.

I have seen past performance and I have mentioned above some of the 'average' results.

My mentor in his 'retirement' has developed a large network of top class traders all around the globe. He has developed a wholesale trading product that is is high demand by many of the wholesale funds, think of this as the funds where the banks play and make a good portion their profits in, and it has been a long term goal of his to make this available to the general public.

I asked him if I was able to mention it in this book, too help spread the message, to which he said "absolutely" On the proviso that I provided some education with regards the FX and how it can work for the people that get introduced to it.

Given that I am all about educating people I thought that to be a no brainer.

With that we have developed a webinar training series that will provide you with the foundations of what you need to become a trader that wins with your trades, at the same time the people that take up the opportunity to get the training will also have the opportunity to utilise the system the I mentioned above.

The beauty and benefits of this are two fold, the first is that you have the opportunity to earn while you learn, and the second is that you, yes *you* have total autonomy and control over your investment, you can draw down, or add to it at anytime, and the fund, if left will continue to compound and grow. It is win/win all around.

To find out more about when the next one of there webinars is, simply go to www.AndrewHawkes.com/FXWebinar and register for the next one. This strategy alone in this book has the potential to provide you the capital needed for you grow and share your message with ease. Don't take my word for it though, go check it out for yourself.

I'LL GIVE YOU FIVE

"Simplicity is the Ultimate Sophistication".
~Leonardo De Vinci

I wanted to add this in here more as a bonus than anything else, it is something that not many people are doing... and I think it is, although a little cheeky, *absolutely brilliant.*

For this to work you don't need to have a lot of website building knowledge, you don't even need to have a product realistically.

You can do a simple search for PLR products, which means Private Label Rights products, these are products that you can purchase the rights to rebrand them, or use them in pretty much anyway that you want... of course you will need to read the license to see what you can do with them, however most of them are pretty flexible.

It could even be something that you know how to do, or something that you are good at that you can do easily… I would recommend you visit the website www.fiverr.com to get some inspiration (this is where we are going to create an income stream from). Basically you are going to write a report that people are going to want to purchase and you are going to make money… or you are going to use the PLR products and sell it there for $5, this is a really quick way to start generating income. The reason I say to create a report or to sell a product is that you are leveraging your work; it is not something that you are you going to be slaving away for each and every time someone orders your 'gig' (because that would NOT be a good use of your time).

If you are going to use a report as your 'gig' (there are examples you can view on fiverr) without doubt it must provide value, and in my mind it must also provide a bigger purpose. Let me break it down for you.

I purchased a report on there that said it could show me a way to make $2,000 a month without using fiver, so I invested the princely sum of $5 and got the report, the report did most certainly show me a way where I could generate a $2,000 a month, there was value in that in itself, however where I think the person fell down was that there was nothing in his report where I could go to get the start that he was talking about.

He missed a golden opportunity to start building a list while getting paid to do so, there are not many places around where you can do that, so take full advantage of it.

You are in effect pre-qualifying your prospects as they are prepared to pay for your report, I get a kick out of it as there are people spending 100's if not 1000's a day on building lists and here I am getting paid for it.

Not only getting paid to build the list, if they like what they see (if it is a report for example), then there is a possibility to convert them into a customer that you are then able to build a relationship with and sell to them over and over again.

It is not the only place that you can use the report either, you can use it pretty much anywhere. Do a search on places you can use them, if you are running a blog and want to build a list (that is related to the report and blog of course) then you can use it as a lead magnet on your blog, the possibilities are endless, let your imagination go nuts!

This chapter was simply to offer a little bonus where you could head out without a website and without a product of your own and start to generate an income... short and sweet.

HOUSE KEEPING

Before we finish up here there are a few 'housekeeping' details to go through.

Some of the things I wanted to house keep are some common misunderstandings, like the wealth paradox and the fact that for all the help and support you can get, you are ultimately on your own. The master of your own destiny.

Common Misunderstandings

"Action is the foundational key to all success".
~Pablo Picasso

Some of the common misunderstandings that I hear a lot about, or that I see, is that there are only a select few that can achieve success, be it online, or offline.

People seem to think that to be successful then they must be born into a successful family (what ever successful means). They see successful people as having some sort of hidden 'success' talent that they themselves do not possess.

What complete and utter horseshit… this could be down to our condition, something that we spoke about in 'The Ugly Truth' however the truth of the matter is that when you break it down, any specific talent or skill only ever comes down to 5-10% of what it takes the be successful, while the remaining 90-95% comes down to attitude, skill be damned!

I invite you to do the exercise yourself to see what I mean; We are going to use a sales person an example here; you can pretty much do this with anything (position) however I am just keeping it simple. So we begin by creating a list of attributes that a sales person needs to be successful, to BE the best sales person in the world, the list could include things like:

Charismatic

Jovial

Persuasive

Honest

Loyal

Passionate

Inviting

Caring

Empathetic

Hard working

Tenacious

You get the idea, this works great when you have more than a 100 words, as it gives you a nice round figure to work with.

Now thinking about these words, and keeping in mind that a *'skill'* is something that you would need a minimum of six months *formal* education in, go through and underline all the words that you believe are 'skills'. If you have done this right… and been very brutally honest, you will be able to see for yourself that what I have written above is correct.

Another common misunderstanding is something that we have mentioned in the last chapter, and that is if there is something that looks too good to be true then it must be.

It is the craziest thing in the world to think that, we have been brainwashed by the media and well-meaning people in our lives to say that something that could be pure and amazing, will more than likely be not real... seriously?

My good friend says, why don't you ever hear anyone say *"oh that is too bad to be true... it can't be"* Yet some of the things you see on television and the internet look 'too bad to be true' and most people believe it to be gospel without giving it a second thought!

Here is another, it's a beauty. That 'if you have money you will be an ass hole' let me tell you, money doesn't make you anything... *you are either an ass hole or you're not.* Money doesn't cause you to be that one day, it simply amplifies what you already are, if you are an asshole then you are now a bigger asshole (with money), if you are an amazing caring person then you just become more able to care and be amazing... get what I am saying?

Money is NOT the root of all evil... *lack* of money is. Enough said.

All of my friends will give me shit or rip me off... are they really your friends if that is the case? Get better friends.

Are you starting to see the trend here... there is a mantra that is bantered about and that is; *'If it is going to be, it is up to me'* learn it, own it, and reap the benefits that come with it.

The Wealth Paradox

"Wealth is not his that has it, but his that enjoys it."
~Benjamin Franklin

I just want to cover the concept of the *'wealth paradox'*, this is my understanding of it and why I think it is important to know what it is.

Wealth is not to be confused with *money*, as so many of us, me included, have thought it was at some stage in our lives.

Wealth is about *much more than money*, it is about the *knowledge* that we have, our financial acumen. For example, I have mentioned people who have won the lottery only to lose everything and then some right? This was down to their lack of financial literacy, had it been higher then they may have kept their money. They were, using our wealth analogy, *poor in knowledge* and knew not how to maintain the money that they had won, or in some cases inherited.

On the flip side of that, if someone who has a great financial literacy, or the desire to increase it, loses all of their money, it does not take them long to reacquire it, that is because they are *wealthy in knowledge* and in mindset that will help them regain what they had lost, after all in many cases they used the knowledge to amass it in the first place.

It has been said that if all the worlds cash was distributed evenly, meaning that we each got an even share, there would be about $9,000 [2]

per man, woman and child, note this is just the cash, not taking into account real estate etc... So, not a huge amount, in most cases people would be worse off than they are now, in relation to that however it is also said that within 20 years (personally I would think sooner than that) the money would be distributed as it is now (rich and poor), and this is due to the level of financial literacy someone has.

I think the most common understanding of the wealth paradox would be that;

The more money that you earn, the more you need to survive.

This is due largely to the fact that most people who earn great incomes, do not necessarily understand how to have that money work for them and have it grow.

The same can be true the other way also, that is if there was someone who didn't earn a big pay cheque however increased their financial literacy and learned how to have their money work for them would soon have true financial independence and *holistic* wealth.

Learning how to develop new incomes streams and have that money coming in is really only the first step.

---

[2] http://www.freemoneyfinance.com/2009/09/all-the-money-in-the-world-divided-equally.html

You will also want to learn how to have that money *working* for you, and this is something that I will look to cover in future books that are released. As with anything that I write however, it is not meant as advice, simply a possibility for you to explore.

I will not be writing about anything that I have not done, or are involved with in some way myself. Like anything, it is always a good idea to investigate it thoroughly and understand it yourself, before actually doing it.

You Are On Your Own

It doesn't have to be all dark and gloomy… all I am saying here is that you have yourself to rely on and that is it. There will be times where you are going to ask questions, that is fine and it is encouraged. I would suggest though that when you ask the question that you ask it of someone who *has the results that you want* (or at the very least someone who *thinks* the same way you do).

The reason is pretty obvious when you think about it, and that is unless they have been where, or done what you want to do, how can they help you?

More often than not you are going to have to trust your own intuition and gut feeling, if you get it wrong, so what, you learned something. As I have said I have not always got it right, however I have never given up, and that is key.

There is also a slightly darker side to this though I suppose, and that is the fact that there are people in your life who care for you, and cherish being in your life, and sometimes it is these people, that you would think would be happy for your success, are in fact the ones that will turn their back on you and tell you that you have changed.

They will most likely come up with all sorts of reasons why you have changed, when the truth is that they, instead of being happy for you, are bitter and envious about what you have created, and this is not because they are jealous and bitter by nature, it is because they are angry at themselves for not getting off their backsides and doing something too.

Everyone, and I mean everyone, has the power to change their circumstances, their lot in life, unfortunately only a few choose to. That is the cold hard truth.

You are on your own, well apart from the 1000's of people and the universe that are conspiring for your success there are a few out there.

FINAL THOUGHTS

Well here we are, at the end of this first book, it was, and is my intention to provide you information that provides you with the necessary tools and expertise that will enable you to generate ever increasing streams of income, and thus enabling you to create true financial freedom and independence.

Some of the ideas I have shared here are not new, however they may be new to you, and even if they were not, then you may very well have seen something that you are able to put your own spin on, to be able to call it your own and own it, and that is great.

Nothing will make me more happy than if you were to go on to do that, and create the lifestyle you are looking for, after all life is for living and having fun, and if you are not doing that then you need to ask yourself *why the hell not*, life is way too short.

There are ideas in here that not everyone will agree with, you know what, I am *OK* with that, there may be things that others do that I don't agree with, luckily we still live in the free world where freedom of speech is encouraged and people are still entitled to their own opinion (well most of us anyway).

All I ask of people is to keep an open mind to what is written here, you know the mind is like a parachute, *it works much better when it is open*. There is no way that this could have been written to please everyone that reads it, nor would I try to.

I am sure that some people have actually purchased this book simply so they can try and pull it to pieces. If that is the case then good luck to them.

We used to have a saying (and I'm sure they still do) in the Air Force that was *"Anyone can do it rough"* this was in regards to the Army as they were always complaining how 'easy' the Air Force had it while on deployments, it was really friendly banter however I believe it to fit quite well here.

What it refers to is that it is easy to complain or to try and pick holes in something; you see, it takes the focus (even if only for a short time) off of their own inadequacies and their own shortcomings.

It gives temporary relief from a life that is not fulfilled or fulfilling for that matter. It provides connection for them and makes them feel important.

The reason I am including what I have just written here is simple, it may sound like a ramble and a rant, however I have worked hard to put this book together, and I know that all I have written in here works, and to the *extent in which* it does.

I am proud of what I have written here and I honestly believe it has the power to change people's lives, even if only by providing another $1,000 a month, it may not seem like much, however to some families and individuals this can be the difference between being on the street or being warm in a house and bed.

I thoroughly enjoyed writing this; even if at times I was like, *"what am I doing?"* it has been one of the most rewarding experiences that I think could have done, I re-read the chapters and learn something, that is powerful in itself.

When you can read something that you yourself, have written and find that you learn something new, it is a crazy, however satisfying feeling and it helps you to understand your true worth.

So here it is. I think we are done. Throughout this book you have seen quotes from famous people who have shaped the world we live in today, well I want to leave you with some words of my own, and that is this;

"We are all perfect vessels of light, we all have a gift to share with the world.... what sets us apart from those that are seemingly 'in the spot light' is the fact that they believe it to be true".
~*Andrew Goldan Hawkes*

NAMASTE

PRAISE FOR RIVERS OF GOLD

"Finally a get real, honest, full of integrity book to take hold, within this there is the boldness of helping many to achieve their dreams, including my own, with ease it takes every-one who will read this to fully understand in what we see miss with reading other such books like this one. Its a guide unto its own. Simplicity and the writer has walked the talk, so to speak! Comes from your knowing and this makes a huge difference for me, and I am sure many more would agree"

Heather Ellis-Drake, The Soul Whisperer.
www.heatherellisdrake.com

"What an honour to give a testimonial for 'Rivers of Gold;How to Create Multiple Income Streams'. It is not only a great read, but one that everyone who would like to change their outcomes in life HAS to read. There are many times throughout our lives we all may think that there are no options to get out of our circumstances available to use, but this is where this book dispels that myth. Take on what you read in 'Rivers of Gold', apply it and watch your outcomes change"

Justin Herald
International Entrepreneur of the Year 2005/06
Author of 8 International Best Selling Books
www.JustinHerald.com

"Just like chewing the fat over a Coffee in East Timor, easy to read and totally conversational"

Geoff Polglase
Real Estate ~ Development & Sales

"What Andrew teaches in this book is not some new get rich quick scheme, in fact it's not new, it is what successful and wealthy people have known for centuries, and kept secret.

Andrew, in his easy to understand style, shows how you can create the life that you want through developing multiple streams of income. The world economy is undergoing tremendous change, many people will suffer needlessly because they don't have, or act on this information, yet for many this will be the greatest opportunity ever presented. I know it works, because it's worked for me and I'm sure if you follow this path you can have the same results as well".

Craig Harwood
Winner Gold Award for Quality
Winner Family Business of The Year Gold Coast Region
Winner Queensland Exporter of the Year
Finalist Australian Exporter of the Year Awards

Founder
www.AustralianWebMarketing.com.au

WOW! What a great read. Andrew has been very open, very honest and very generous with the information that he used personally to succeed in his own life. Rivers of Gold is a step by step manual that if you apply it you will succeed too. This is a highly recommended read for all people who personally want to Win at the game of Wealth!

Stacey Huish
Founder
www.generational-change-foundation.org

ABOUT THE AUTHOR

Andrew Hawkes is father to three beautiful children, and loving husband to his beautiful wife Sarah. They reside on the Gold Coast of Australia.

Andrew has known from a very young age that there was something different about the way he looked at life, never one to settle on the status quo he has always been driven to the next challenge in his life. In doing so Andrew has developed a skill in reading people and helping them to identify areas of their life where they can and would like to improve, be it financial, spiritual, and physical or within a relationship. Andrew is now in demand for his 'to the point' briefs and strategies.

At the age of four Andrew was involved in his first entrepreneurial activity when, not satisfied with the lucky dip he had one, and having no money to buy another, he set about to sell the original, not only did he sell it, he sold it for twice the original amount.

This began a continuing trend at at 14 he successfully negotiated, then subsequently subcontracted, drainage work whilst his home town was connected to the sewer system.

Andrew is passionate about assisting people to regain more of their own person connection to source energy and the non physical. Andrew has honed and continues to refine his own personal connection to source and regularly receives 'givings' from a non-physical guide who has identified themselves as 'Zoran' which comes has a Persian origin.

Andrew speaks on the topics of 'Personal Attraction' and 'Spiritual Intuition'. He believes that everyone has an access to the non physical, a connection to source, and that signals and signs come sometimes in the most subtle of ways. It was only after years of having these signals, and having a catalyst to activate them all in reverse, connecting the dots looking back, that he was able to piece it all together and finally understand what his purpose here in this life time was for.

Meet Andrew and find out more about him at

www.AndrewHawkes.com

RESOURCES

The 10 Step Money System

This is the Simple Process that I followed (and continue to follow) To Recover from Bankruptcy

Take Control of Your Money NOW

www.AndrewHawkes.com/free-resources/

Your Powerful Intention Audio

Download this Audio Free at

www.AndrewHawkes.com/free-resources/

Quantum Connection Podcast

Listen to Andrew on his Quantum Connection Podcast. Find archive episodes and subscribe to the regular episodes.

www.AndrewHawkes.com/podcast/

www.ingramcontent.com/pod-product-compliance
Lightning Source LLC
Chambersburg PA
CBHW071622170426
43195CB00038B/1762